RECORDING THE CLASSICS

Recording the Classics

Maestros, Music,
and
Technology

ᔑ

JAMES BADAL

THE KENT STATE UNIVERSITY PRESS

Kent, Ohio, and London, England

© 1996 by The Kent State University Press, Kent, Ohio 44242
All rights reserved
Library of Congress Catalog Card Number 95-35978
ISBN 0-87338-542-X
Manufactured in the United States of America

04 03 02 01 00 99 98 97 96   5 4 3 2 1

Library of Congress Cataloging-in-Publication Data

Recording the classics : maestros, music, and technology / James Badal
    [interviewer].
      p.   cm.
    Includes bibliographical references.
    ISBN 0-87338-542-x (cloth : alk. paper) ∞
    1. Conductors—Interviews. 2. Performance practice (Music)—20th century. 3. Sound
    recordings—Social aspects. 4. Sound recording industry.
    ML402.R43 1996   95-35978
    781.49—dc20   CIP
                                                   MN

British Library Cataloging-in-Publication data are available.

To my mother

Elizabeth B. Badal

CONTENTS

PREFACE

～

THIS SERIES OF conversations originally grew out of a professional journalism assignment. As a contributing editor to the arts magazine *Northern Ohio Live,* I interviewed Lorin Maazel in 1981 about his recording activities with the Cleveland Orchestra; portions of that discussion subsequently appeared in the November issue. Some of the questions explored or touched on during that conversation struck me as particularly significant, especially since there seemed to be little discussion in print of the impact records and recording have had on musical culture. Over the next nine years, I therefore arranged as many interviews as possible with visiting conductors through the Cleveland Orchestra's marketing and public relations department at Severance Hall. All of the interviews since that first one with Maazel appeared in the record-review magazine *Fanfare* between 1984 and 1991.

I owe a debt of gratitude to John T. Hubbell, director of The Kent State University Press, and to my editor, Julia J. Morton, for both their enthusiasm and their patient, constant support while this book was being put together.

Thanks also to John Shambach, publisher of *Northern Ohio Live,* and Joel Flegler, publisher of *Fanfare,* for permission to reprint previously published material.

I am indebted to several generations of the Severance Hall marketing and public relations staff. Jan C. Snow, Rick Lester, and Gary Hanson not only squeezed interviews into conductors' tight rehearsal schedules but convinced some major musicians that a discussion with an unknown, local writer would not be a waste of time.

Several people were instrumental in helping me compile the photographs that appear in this book. I especially thank Carol S. Jacobs (archivist),

Sue Sackman, Rosie Withem, and Debbie Clark at Severance Hall in Cleveland. Thanks also to John Eustace at WEA, Dennis Tolly at Columbia Artists Management, Inc., Odette Gélinas at the Orchestre Symphonique de Montréal, Gary Reider and Elaine Martone at Telarc International Corporation, Jennifer Perciballi at EMI, Shaw Concerts, Inc., and the New York Philharmonic.

Peter Hastings photographed Cleveland Orchestra personnel and guests for thirty years. In 1981, he published many of his wonderful pictures in *Musical Images*. I am delighted that eight of the photographs that appear in this book are his.

AUTHOR'S NOTE

ﾞﾞﾞﾞﾞ

FOR THE MOST part, I refer to record companies only in passing. I have therefore made no attempt to disentangle the history of various business alliances, takeovers, and changes in company names. My use of label names has been casual but consistent. I assume anyone interested enough to read these interviews will know that English Decca is known as London in the United States, that HMV stands for His Master's Voice, and that Columbia later became CBS and eventually Sony.

INTRODUCTION

⁂

THERE IS A STORY, perhaps apocryphal, about a young journalist who reported on the first public demonstrations of television at the RCA pavilion during the 1939 New York World's Fair. Though deeply impressed by the new medium, he wrote an article in which he predicted that this invention, miraculous though it was, would never replace radio in the public's affections because no one would have time for it. After all, he reasoned, a listener could turn on the radio and go about his or her business in the home, but a potential viewer would have to sit in front of the television for the duration of the program. Who would have time for this?

It is the sort of story the late media theorist Marshall McLuhan would have eagerly seized upon, for it—together with TV's subsequent history—clearly demonstrates one of his central theses: the most powerful effects a medium has on society occur gradually over a long period and are never the ones that are most obvious. For example, when we debate the great issues of television, we focus on such matters as sex and violence in prime time and advertisements aimed at children; rarely do we discuss the degree to which television has molded the patterns of our lives. Studies have indicated, however, that the average American TV set is on between six and seven hours per day; on Superbowl Sunday, the entire country turns into a coast-to-coast ghost town; in the pre–video cassette recorder world, we adjusted mealtimes and social obligations around the TV; streets emptied when *M*A*S*H** bowed out and when *Dallas* revealed who shot J. R. Ewing; studies even suggest that as a nation we sleep less now than in the years before TV became such a prominent player in our lives. Somehow, somewhere—in spite of that reporter's prediction—we have found the time for television.

Though the medium may be quite different, the situation with recordings is similar. When we ask what benefits have been derived from recordings, we generally supply ourselves with a series of music appreciation answers.

Recordings have increased the general public's knowledge and sophistication in the area of classical music; they bring noteworthy performances of fine music to those who might have little access to live concerts; they allow listeners to become familiar with music rarely heard in the concert hall or opera house; and they preserve the work of great artists from the past and present.

But have recordings also affected how the public perceives music or even the way musicians make it? Because of recordings, do listeners come to the concert hall with a certain set of aural expectations? (In one ludicrously extreme case, as relayed by an assistant head usher at Severance Hall, a disgruntled concertgoer complained bitterly that, contrary to what a salesman had told him, the Cleveland Orchestra "highs" were different live than from his speakers!) Does recorded music in any way create erroneous impressions of either the music or the performer?

Some of these issues did surface in the early days of the medium. Among the first great conductors to record was the legendary Arthur Nikisch. In 1913, companies from England and Germany teamed up to record Beethoven's Fifth Symphony with Nikisch and the Berlin Philharmonic, the first recording of a complete symphony ever made and one that both EMI and Deutsche Grammophon have reissued over the years to celebrate various anniversaries. Even allowing for the severe restrictions imposed by the acoustic recording process, the performance just does not sound like the work of the wild, flamboyant magician described by those, including George Szell,[1] who saw him in the concert hall. Have distant, fading memories led to exaggerated reports, or did Nikisch simply conduct differently on those few occasions he recorded?

In a similar manner, Richard Strauss's formidable reputation as a conductor is ill served by at least part of his recorded legacy. Cynics would maintain that his interest in making records was financial rather than artistic. Clearly there were occasions in the studio when he was engaged neither emotionally nor intellectually, and it is difficult to reconcile some of the perfunctory performances he left with the magnitude of his reputation.

Karl Muck possessed an astonishingly wide orchestral and operatic repertoire. Though fiercely conservative in his tastes, he presented music that he personally disliked, and in some cases did not fully understand, during his tenure with the Boston Symphony in the years immediately

---

1. Harold C. Schonberg, *The Great Conductors* (New York: Simon and Schuster, 1967), 215.

before World War I.[2] The public, however, associated him primarily with Wagner—partially because he conducted *Parsifal* at Bayreuth from 1901 to 1930, partially because of his startling physical and temperamental resemblance to the composer. Muck also recorded a legendary series of Wagner performances between 1927 and 1929, including a virtually complete third act of *Parsifal* in 1928. Except for some Berlioz, Tchaikovsky, Wolf-Ferrari, and Beethoven with the Boston Symphony in 1917, he recorded no other composer. Ironically, one of the most versatile performing musicians is therefore remembered in the public mind almost exclusively as a Wagner conductor.

Among the conductors born in the middle of the nineteenth century, Felix Weingartner was one of the most prolific in the studio, and in his case, the body of recorded material accurately reflects his interests, strengths, and skills as a conductor. The one-time Liszt pupil recorded the music of his teacher as well as complete cycles of Beethoven and Brahms symphonies. (He was the first to record all nine Beethoven symphonies.) Contemporary reports indicated that the drama of opera eluded him, and he wisely avoided the musical theater when he recorded, save for a few overtures, preludes, and other orchestral tidbits. Oddly, considering his impeccable credentials in the classical symphonic repertoire, he recorded no Haydn and only one Mozart symphony, No. 39 (but he recorded it no fewer than four times).

Any recording, even a heavily edited studio product, represents an artist's interpretation of that work at that moment in time. In essence, it is an audio snapshot. Indeed, a number of the conductors interviewed here use the terms *photograph* or *picture* to describe recordings. Judgments of individual performances or overall impressions of a musician are conditioned by the number and nature of the "photographs" available. The recording industry generally celebrates the new and the technologically up-to-date; therefore, when a conductor has made multiple versions of the same work, the newest will usually survive in the company catalogue. If most serious listeners think of Bruno Walter as warm, genial, even saintly, it is largely because his stereo remakes of Beethoven, Brahms, and Mozart with the Columbia Symphony remain more readily available than their older, monophonic, more volatile counterparts. There are, of course, exceptions. All four of Herbert von Karajan's commercially recorded Beethoven symphony cycles were available as of July 1994, five years after his death, thus affording

2. Schonberg, *Great Conductors,* 220.

an opportunity to study the evolution of his approach to this repertoire over a period of more than three decades.

Recordings can create particularly erroneous impressions of conductors born late in the nineteenth century, because judgment is often based only on those performances produced at the end of a long career. When Toscanini made his first recordings with the orchestra of La Scala in 1921 at the Camden, New Jersey, studio of the Victor Talking Machine Company (later RCA Victor), he was fifty-three years old, and fully one-half of his professional career, about thirty-four years, already lay behind him. Of the earlier period, we have absolutely no aural evidence. The fiercely demanding maestro contemptuously dismissed this small collection of acoustically recorded, sonically dismal tidbits. Thereafter, he visited recording studios sporadically until his association with the NBC Symphony began during his seventieth year in 1937. The vast bulk of the commercially available Toscanini material dates from roughly the last decade of his career—the late 1940s to his retirement in 1954 at the age of eighty-seven. Over the years, commentators, especially those immune or indifferent to Toscanini's powers, have characterized these documents of the maestro's old age as overly rigid, overly fast, and overly tense; yet a very different picture emerges from a comparison of the late NBC material with the small handfuls of commercial discs made with the New York Philharmonic and BBC Symphony Orchestra in the 1930s, the Philadelphia recordings of 1941–42 (not available in their entirety until 1976), the 1937 Salzburg performances of *Die Zauberflöte, Die Meistersinger,* and *Falstaff,* as well as all the various legal and pirated issues of live concerts, including those from the early NBC years. Recently EMI released a 1935 live BBC performance of the prelude to act 1 of *Parsifal,* a performance of such deliberation and flexibility that it suddenly seems credible that Toscanini did indeed preside over the slowest *Parsifal* in Bayreuth history.

The general perception of Otto Klemperer's music-making is similarly distorted, and for identical reasons. The great German conductor recorded very little until EMI's legendary producer Walter Legge teamed him with London's Philharmonia Orchestra in the mid-1950s. By then Klemperer was in his seventies and had survived a daunting series of personal trials ranging from exile to brain surgery. His style had solidified (some would say ossified) into a relatively predictable pattern: sometimes grandly monumental, occasionally just ponderous. As Simon Rattle pointed out during my interview with him, however, interested listeners who have access to the (admittedly scanty) documentation of Klemperer in his pre-EMI days will hear an entirely different conductor. Though a certain austerity and seriousness of purpose characterize all his music-making, his discs with the Vienna Symphony from the early 1950s, the live material from his Budapest days in the late 1940s, and the few studio-made recordings from the 1920s reveal a fiery temperament rarely glimpsed in his later EMI endeavors.

Klemperer's contemporary image is further molded by the standard bread-and-butter, Bach-through-Mahler repertoire he recorded for EMI. For a listening public that links him with such guardians of tradition as Wilhelm Furtwängler, Hans Knappertsbusch, and Bruno Walter, it remains hard to believe that as director of Berlin's Kroll during the Weimar Republic, he outraged conservative tastes by performing works by Janáček, Krenek, and Schoenberg, and by producing avant-garde stagings of such popular favorites as Wagner's *Der Fliegende Holländer.*

Working successfully in the studio requires an understanding of the role recordings play in contemporary musical life, as well as enough technical literacy to be comfortable with the process of making them. Though such skills may be simple enough for conductors born into an environment in which recordings have always existed, for their elder colleagues, the studio remained a totally alien world. In the era of acoustical recording, the studio forced musicians to crowd uncomfortably in front of a large horn. The early days of electrical recording presented a world of machines, wires, and microphones, of distressingly short takes, of constant starting and stopping. The conductor was obliged to try to capture the sense of a public performance with no public present. Worst of all, the sonic results were hardly gratifying.

Many famous conductors of the past were understandably unfamiliar with recording technology and failed to grasp the significance recordings could have. According to his biographer, Hans-Hubert Schönzeler, Furtwängler never fully understood the value of a recording until he recorded Wagner's *Tristan und Isolde* for EMI in 1952, though he labored in the studio from 1925 until his death in 1954.[3] Producer John Culshaw related that Hans Knappertsbusch refused to listen to the playback of the first major take when he recorded act 1 of Wagner's *Die Walküre* for London in 1957; rather, he sat alone, serenely smoking a cigarette while cast and crew

---

3. Hans-Hubert Schönzeler, *Furtwängler* (Portland, Ore.: Amadeus, 1990), 151.

headed for the control room.[4] Apparently Klemperer registered genuine shock when told that a minor mistake in an otherwise exemplary take could be corrected during editing. The aging giant reportedly turned a despairing face to his daughter Lotte and proclaimed such technical trickery *"ein Schwindel."*

Toscanini's epic battles with everything connected with the medium have assumed legendary status. Violinist Samuel Antek remembered that RCA installed a small speaker at the foot of the maestro's podium so technicians in the control room could communicate with him easily. When Toscanini heard a voice issuing from the tiny box, he would bend over and speak back into it, almost, suggested Antek, as if he assumed a little man resided inside.[5] A scene from the famous 1943 U.S. Office of War Information film called for Toscanini to place a 78 rpm record on the spindle of his phonograph. When the film is shown publicly today, record buffs in the audience invariably giggle and groan as the maestro mauls the fragile disc like a champion discus thrower. Both Samuel Chotzinoff and B. H. Haggin have attested to Toscanini's clumsiness while handling his own records, the latter's description of gouged discs and damaged styli being especially eloquent.[6] Haggin also remembered that the maestro would sometimes listen to recordings with treble and bass controls turned to the maximum in an apparent attempt to wring every last ounce of sound from a sonically imperfect document.[7]

There were, however, conductors born in the last years of the nineteenth century who managed quite well with recordings. Leopold Stokowski's career-long interest in records and recording technology led him to make some remarkable stereophonic experiments at the Bell Laboratories in the early 1930s and to embrace the sonic razzle-dazzle of London's Phase 4 techniques in the 1960s. Even though Bruno Walter was in virtual retirement by the late fifties, Columbia lured him back into the studio to rerecord much of his basic repertoire in stereo. Based on the evidence of the substantial rehearsal material that has been in circulation, the eighty-some-year-old conductor adjusted to studio conditions far more successfully than many of his contemporaries.

4. John Culshaw, *Ring Resounding* (New York: Viking, 1967), 69.

5. Samuel Antek, *This Was Toscanini* (New York: Vanguard, 1963), 113.

6. Samuel Chotzinoff, *Toscanini: An Intimate Portrait* (New York: Knopf, 1956), 141; B. H. Haggin, *Conversations with Toscanini* (Garden City, N.Y.: Doubleday, 1959), 149.

7. Haggin, *Conversations with Toscanini*, 30.

Relative youth is, however, no real guarantee of technical literacy or comfort in the studio. According to rumor, one major conductor cast two vocal lightweights in a major opera recording because he thought digital technology would transform their voices to make them sound more heroic.

In the concert hall and the opera house, the conductor controls every aspect of the performance; the dynamics, the balances, and the tempi proceed from his understanding of the score, coupled with his assessment of the venue's acoustical properties. Recording takes away a portion of that autocratic control in several ways, not least by allotting power to the producer and the producer's technical team. Responsible for setting up and running the sessions, the producer determines the character of the recorded sound in consultation with the conductor.

During much of industry history, the producer remained unknown to the general public. Even today, for most consumers, he is simply one name among many listed in the credits of a CD booklet. A few producers, such as EMI's Walter Legge and London's John Culshaw, have managed to achieve considerable fame. Legge gave Karajan's career a significant boost in the immediate postwar years by bringing him to London and the newly created Philharmonia Orchestra. Today, Culshaw is remembered almost exclusively for his work in opera. Part technical wizard, part music-loving philosopher, he argued that modern recording technology should be used freely and fully to create an ideal sound stage, including aurally dramatic effects clearly called for in the score or suggested in the action but virtually impossible to realize during the hubbub of actual performance. With the active cooperation of such major figures as Georg Solti and Herbert von Karajan, Culshaw put his theories into practice during the late fifties and sixties, producing a legendary series of sonically spectacular opera recordings that included the first commercial *Ring* cycle. The issue of Strauss's *Elektra,* one of the more extreme examples of Culshaw's art, provoked *High Fidelity*'s Conrad L. Osborne to challenge the validity of his assumptions, thus touching off a famous aesthetic debate between the two in the magazine's pages.

The relationship between conductor and producer is an artistic partnership in the best sense of the term, and since preserving the performance as attractively and effectively as possible remains a significant part of the producer's job, he must be something of a musician himself. Not all such marriages are happy. In the waning days of Lorin Maazel's tenure with the Cleveland Orchestra, rumors began to surface about an explosive exchange between the maestro and his CBS producer during the sessions for Berlioz's

Symphonie fantastique which resulted in Maazel polishing off the piece as quickly as possible and refusing to listen to the playbacks. The interview with Maazel included in this book took place roughly at the time of this confrontation, when his rage was clearly still simmering.

There have been some astonishing mismatches between a conductor's "sound" and the acoustical environment provided by the producer and the recording team. George Szell favored a lean, hard-edged orchestra sonority, precise attacks, and sharp accents. Ideally, this astringent palette would require a sense of warmth and space around it, a sonic cushion to show the performance off to best advantage. Instead, Columbia and its Epic subsidiary provided a tight, constricted sonic environment that exaggerated the hallmarks of Szell's style; while it served Haydn and Mozart, as well as some twentieth-century scores reasonably well, it could be distinctly unflattering to Szell's conceptions of Brahms, Wagner, Strauss, and even Beethoven.

Herbert von Karajan suffered a similar technical mismatch with EMI during the late fifties and early sixties. The well-known characteristics of the Karajan style—the smooth, luxurious blended sonorities; the seamless, effortless flow; the rounded contours—demanded a sound picture emphasizing clarity: the sort of acoustic Deutsche Grammophon provided him through the sixties and seventies. Instead, EMI produced a nebulous, murky sound (at least on the evidence of their American Angel releases of the late 1950s and early 1960s) that turned his performances into sonic mush.

Since no recording can be issued without the conductor having approved the final tape, perhaps even the resulting LP or CD, it seems inconceivable that any discerning musician would let pass a sonically butchered job, even granting the fact that not all listen equally well with technological ears. Many of these sonically problematic Szell and Karajan performances are currently available on CD, and the remastering reveals that at least in some cases, the engineering faults rested not so much with the original recording job as with the subsequent processing.

It is astonishing the degree to which the sonic characteristics of a recording can be altered. In the past, both Deutsche Grammophon and Philips recordings appeared on LPs manufactured and distributed by American companies: the former by American Decca, the later by Mercury. In both cases, noisy disc surfaces, a constricted dynamic range, and generally muffled sound made accurate assessment and enjoyment of the performances difficult. The inferiority of the American product became shockingly evident when both companies abandoned the local middlemen and began distributing European-manufactured discs—with their silent surfaces and cleaner, fuller sound—in the United States. The interpretations preserved on those immaculate German and Dutch pressings seemed better, even greater, than the identical performances on poorer, domestically manufactured discs.

In 1963 the London label recorded *Carmen* in Vienna under Karajan. For contractual reasons, RCA released the set in the United States while in Germany Telefunken-manufactured discs were issued in RCA boxes. On Telefunken, the overture in Karajan's hands explodes with thunderously brilliant cymbal crashes and sharp, powerful tympani blows. On RCA LPs the aggressive maestro suddenly turns civilized and genteel, the cymbals somewhat muted, the tympani strokes soft and a little tubby.

During my interview with Erich Leinsdorf, he complained about RCA's Dynagroove—a process utilized by the company during his Boston Symphony days in the 1960s—because he felt it severely distorted the dynamics of the original recordings. Newer European issues, he reported with a certain wonder, had, according to acquaintances, corrected the sonic aberrations he found so offensive.

In a posh Los Angeles record store a number of years ago, the discerning collector in search of Wagner's *Rienzi* on EMI could choose among British, French, and German LP issues of the same performance. To a record buff, this is not simply an example of Rodeo Drive–inspired extravagance, for the truly knowledgeable collector could discourse at length on the subtle and not-so-subtle sonic variations among the sets.

The digital and CD revolutions appear to have solved some of the problems associated with this particular issue. Although different releases of the same performance can reveal variations in the nature of the sound, sonic differences based solely on the country of manufacture do not seem to be the problem with compact discs that they were with long-playing records.

Producers and musicians must have nightmares thinking of the infinite variety of possible sonic mutilations due to differences in playback equipment and home listening environments. John Culshaw complained to a journalist who had criticized the London release of *Tristan und Isolde* for insufficient bass, only to discover the befuddled reviewer played his records on a machine with the bass controls turned down and treble controls turned up to the maximum.[8]

8. Culshaw, *Ring Resounding*, 210–11.

About twenty-five years ago, Deutsche Grammophon recorded all the Beethoven symphonies with Raphael Kubelik. Perhaps to give the set some visibility in a market glutted with Beethoven cycles, the company added a gimmick: nine separate orchestras from all over the world were employed, a different ensemble with each symphony. Interestingly, the differences among the various orchestras were not as striking as perhaps one would have thought. Another quarter-century before then, the national characteristics of orchestras had been much more pronounced. Did recordings play any role in this apparent homogenization?

Similarly, the wide interpretive range evident in the recordings of Toscanini, Mengelberg, Koussevitzky, Stokowski, Rodzinski, Furtwängler, Walter, Beecham, and so on seems to have narrowed considerably in the discs recorded by succeeding generations of conductors. Is this standardization merely a function of changing aesthetic principles, or are recordings establishing interpretive norms?

As some of the conductors interviewed indicate, a youthful encounter with a "special" recording can continue to live in the memory. In a conversation not included in this book, Klaus Tennstedt remembers listening to the Stokowski-Philadelphia Tchaikovsky Fifth with his father in bed under the covers because the Nazis had placed a ban on all Russian music.

One of the classic debates in the industry pits proponents of studio recording against supporters of "live" recording. On the one hand, the studio holds out the promise of perfection: a note-perfect rendition in which every important voice can be heard, carefully assembled from a series of takes of varying length. In opera, a singer can attack the most daunting roles in the repertoire at full throttle, secure in the knowledge that he or she will not tire, fluffs can be repaired, and the voice will always be heard even against the most thunderous orchestral explosions. On the other hand, the live recording promises the excitement of a unique event and the moments of tension and inspiration that can only occur during a complete performance in front of an audience. Christopher Hogwood relishes working in the studio, eagerly embracing the opportunities for experimentation that it offers. Leonard Bernstein, however, after years of successful work in Columbia studios as chief of the New York Philharmonic, came to feel that the live concert situation suited him better.

Some conductors and their recording teams have found inventive ways of combining the studio with the concert hall. Reportedly, Otto Klemperer polished off some symphonies and concertos in one huge take, a practice that Simon Rattle has also come to espouse. When Karl Böhm recorded

Tristan und Isolde for Deutsche Grammophon at Bayreuth in 1966, the opera was performed one act at a time over a three-day period before a specially invited audience, thus preserving the unique Bayreuth acoustics and the intensity of a live performance while ensuring that Wolfgang Windgassen could tackle Tristan's lengthy act 3 delirium in fresh voice.[9]

A related issue involves the question of whether conductors, either by design or inadvertently, produce different kinds of performances in the studio than in the hall. Klemperer's live recordings vary little in interpretation from his studio efforts; Furtwängler's differ considerably. Though some of Furtwängler's concert performances manage to preserve the fierce individuality and extraordinary electricity he could generate in the hall, they do not bear up as well under repeated hearings as his less extreme studio readings. Are certain kinds of performances therefore more phonogenic than others? Are certain performers more phonogenic than others?

For many musicians, recordings become a way of achieving fame and perhaps preserving some of it for after their death. On his eightieth birthday in 1954, Bruno Walter expressed his happiness that recordings guaranteed that all traces of a performing musician's life would not die with him.[10] Some conductors, such as Leonard Bernstein and Eugene Ormandy, have left huge recorded legacies; in the final years of his life, Herbert von Karajan seemed almost obsessed with flooding the market with as many representations of his audio and visual image as his declining health would allow. Today, the Estonian maestro Neeme Järvi appears well on his way to becoming the most heavily recorded conductor in history.

Yet the dynamics of achieving fame through intensive studio activity remain fickle, for the history of the industry is dotted with performers who achieved a measure of renown with few recordings. Fritz Busch's considerable reputation rests almost exclusively on his Glyndebourne-based recordings of the three Mozart–Da Ponte operas made by HMV from 1934 to 1936. Hans Knappertsbusch owes his continuing stature to multiple versions— two commercial, at least three pirated—of one work: Wagner's *Parsifal*. Victor de Sabata enjoys an enormous reputation on the basis of a single recording. The Italian maestro's success in what collectors usually refer to as "the first Callas *Tosca*" of 1953 remains so decisive that had he never recorded another note, his fame would still be assured.

9. Karl Böhm, *A Life Remembered*, trans. John Kehoe (London: Marion Boyers, 1992), 102–3.

10. Bruno Walter, *Bruno Walter in Conversation with Arnold Michaels* (Columbia Masterworks).

And then there is the odd case of Sergiu Celibidache, the Romanian-born conductor who has won notoriety by refusing to record anything at all. Branding recordings as musical falsifications, he ceased all studio activity in the early 1950s. Though he has remained steadfast in his convictions, more recently he has given his blessing to video discs and video cassettes of his concerts—as long as the audio portion is not released separately on CD.

The ability of any conductor to make recordings depends in part on the bottom line: do his recordings sell? I once read that Karajan, Solti, and Bernstein were the only conductors whose discs could be guaranteed to sell in quantity, the implication perhaps being that this economic reality gave them the power to record anything they wished. Though his 1970 version of *Die Zauberflöte* ranks among the best, Solti decided he wanted to record the opera again in 1990. Though committing a major opera to tape requires a much greater investment in time and money than simply rerecording a Beethoven symphony, London bowed to Solti's wishes. Does any major label say no to a top-selling artist who has recorded for the company for over thirty years and also happens to be the all-time Grammy-winning champ?

Karajan, however, ran into trouble when Deutsche Grammophon balked at his desire to record a four-LP set of music by Schoenberg, Berg, and Webern. Those who controlled the pursestrings acquiesced only when the maestro paid for the project himself.[11] That the set turned into a financial success is a tribute to the commercial power of Karajan's name, not to a newfound public interest in the Second Viennese School.

On the other hand, in my interview with Erich Leinsdorf, he bemoans his inability to interest major labels in some admittedly esoteric projects that especially interested him. In this case, economic concerns triumphed over artistic considerations. No matter what the repertoire, all Leinsdorf's name on a record sleeve or CD booklet guarantees is a high degree of professionalism, not high sales.

Recordings also serve as public relations documents and marketing tools, commodities to keep extra cash flowing into orchestra coffers, the ideal vehicles to extend the reputations of both ensemble and conductor beyond the boundaries of their home base. When major symphony orchestras go through the grueling process of searching for a new music director, candidates' ability to bring a recording contract to the organization weighs al-

11. Richard Osborne, *Conversations with Von Karajan* (New York: Harper & Row, 1989), 120.

most as heavily as solid musical credentials. Apparently Zubin Mehta floundered in New York partially because the Philharmonic's recording activities dwindled to almost nothing during his tenure. As Charles Dutoit suggests during our interview, those musicians who do not record have "careers a little hidden."

From a marketing perspective, a constant, steady stream of new releases is ideal. One Severance Hall executive registered his lack of concern when I informed him some of Dohnányi's initial London recordings with the Cleveland Orchestra had been cut from the catalogue, because there was such a backlog of fresh material awaiting release.

Management, conductor, and label must also deal with vexing questions of what repertoire to record, an especially difficult dilemma for a younger musician trying to establish name recognition in a crowded CD market. Is it wise from either an economic or artistic standpoint for relatively green, little-known talent to tackle Beethoven and Brahms symphonies when every major conductor beginning with Arthur Nikisch has placed a personal stamp on this music? And if mainstream repertoire is to be avoided, how far into the fringes should one venture?

These interviews do not reveal definitive answers to such questions. I had no particular ideological positions to defend when I began this project in 1981; my intention was to explore the issues with people who constantly have to grapple with them as part of their professional lives.

All the conversations took place when the conductor involved was appearing with the Cleveland Orchestra in Ohio, either in Severance Hall or at the Blossom Music Center. Our meetings had to be squeezed in among rehearsals, meals, semiofficial duties, even other interviews; time was always a terrible problem, especially during the tightly scheduled summer season at Blossom. The question I include in almost every interview about the public accepting a certain level of technology but seeing danger in further progress seemed a handy way of bringing the conversation to a close— though in some instances, it obviously provoked further discussion.

I present the interviews here in chronological order. When I spoke with Lorin Maazel in 1981, he had already produced his first spectacular digital LPs for Telarc, and the medium of the compact disc stood on the horizon. Taken in the order in which they occurred, these discussions provide an ongoing commentary on the developing digital revolution and subsequent CD explosion.

The interviews are reproduced more or less as they happened, minus a few potentially libelous remarks. Grammatical slips have been corrected, but every attempt has been made to preserve individual usages and phrasings. Throughout, my aim was to allow each conductor to make his points in his own way and to preserve insofar as possible the flavor of the individuals in conversation. There are, no doubt, statements the conductors involved would love to modify or take back entirely. Like the recorded performances with which they are concerned, however, these interviews represent specific moments in time—snapshots of the speakers' thoughts, attitudes, and opinions.

LORIN MAAZEL

❧

BEFORE LORIN MAAZEL came to Cleveland in 1972 as George Szell's successor, he had recorded with a variety of ensembles for a number of major labels. Most of his significant pre-Cleveland studio work, however, had been for London, and the company—apparently eager to expand its activities in the United States—followed the young American maestro to the shores of Lake Erie, just as it had followed Zubin Mehta to Los Angeles in 1967 and Georg Solti to Chicago in 1969.

In addition to this new relationship, the orchestra continued its long-standing association with Columbia, and Maazel divided the obligatory sets of Brahms and Beethoven symphonies between the two labels. His interest in new recording technologies also led him to establish a partnership with Cleveland-based Telarc, an alliance that produced a direct-to-disc effort in the waning days of analog technology and then the company's first digital recordings with a major ensemble.

Maazel has always demonstrated a flare for the dramatic, as well as a touch of the maverick. During his career, he has allied himself with both major and minor labels and has worked on an astonishingly wide range of projects. His eclectic recorded repertoire embraces everything from *Don Giovanni* to *Porgy and Bess,* from Bach and Debussy to Zemlinsky and Andrew Lloyd Webber. Interestingly, his short-lived directorship of the Vienna State Opera yielded only a single recording, a live taping of Puccini's *Turandot.*

I interviewed Lorin Maazel in October of 1981 during his final season in Cleveland. Despite rumors alleging that a virtual state of war existed between the angry, departing maestro and the board of trustees, he appeared calm, relaxed, and thoughtful. Even at the time, his projections of his future recording activities seemed overly optimistic, and though he has worked steadily in the studio since leaving Cleveland, I doubt he has produced recordings in the numbers he suggests here. ❧

London producer Michael Woolcock *(center)* and Lorin Maazel *(right)* at a recording session for Gershwin's *Porgy and Bess* in August 1975. Photo by Peter Hastings. Courtesy of the Archives of the Musical Arts Association/the Cleveland Orchestra.

BADAL: Maestro, conductors of your generation seem to accept recordings fairly readily; yet the older generations, men like Toscanini and Furtwängler, hated the process and hated the results.

MAAZEL: Undoubtedly, they were affected by problems of sound reproduction. It really was quite awful at that time, what with the 78. You see, they could never get more than five minutes per movement on a side. And five minutes of the first movement of the Brahms whatever or the Beethoven whatever was the amount you could get through. You'd have to blend out and then blend in to the spot you'd left off at on the other side of the recording. That's hardly satisfactory to a musician. Just unthinkable! But with the advent of the long play, 33, you got to the point where you could put most normal-length works on one side of the recording. And that changed—that and high fidelity and then stereo—that changed everything. I can't imagine life without recorded sound.

BADAL: What value do you think recordings have?

MAAZEL: Well, assuming the recording represents the view of the work held by the interpreter at that time—a view developed over a period of years in the concert hall—the recording does become a kind of document. As a document of the interpreter's view of the work, it is very precious indeed. Assuming the interpreter has something to say, such documentations have value. I find recording an extremely important part of our cultural life today. I can't imagine not having recorded sound at my disposal. And I'm a professional musician and don't listen to as many recordings as music lovers would. I don't have the time; and when I do listen, it's usually for professional reasons—to familiarize myself with a work I haven't heard, some odd or offbeat affair, or more likely with the interpretation of an artist I've never heard live. The recorded music I listen to when it's a question of enjoying an evening, that is usually recorded music in fields other than my own. And I can't imagine listening to the imperial court music in Japan—having to go there and listen, hear it, as I have, and then not have the opportunity of being able to hear that music someplace else at some other time. It's true of classical music or whatever—to be able to put that recording on, on your terrace on a summer evening; it's absolutely marvelous. I just can't imagine that there would be any overriding reason not to record. Having said that, everything has its place. The live performance has in no way been affected negatively by the recorded one.

BADAL: Some say that live performances *have* been adversely affected by recordings.

MAAZEL: Well, I think a live performance can only be positively affected, if I can draw upon my own experience in this matter. The microphone is a great monster. It tells you everything. The impression the younger artist has, and must have, of his performance—the very nature of the subjectivity in which he prepared his view, developed his very fresh, green, young view—makes it absolutely impossible for him to grasp the true effect of his performance on the listener. It is the task of the performer to project a view of the work. He can't do so unless he's effectively projecting, "effectively" meaning translating into true terms, practical terms, his inherent, felt, intuitive view of the work. That requires finding the proper technical means to express what he wants to say. He may think that he has found them. More often than not, in microphone terms, he hasn't. If he's an intelligent artist—and many aren't and therefore fall by the wayside—he will note there's a discrepancy between what he wants to say and what's been said. He'll try to find out just why that's happening. He hears it one way, and the result is quite different. Listening to his first effort, he begins to discover that there's only one way to be efficient in artistic projection. I use that word advisedly, and I know it may sound very shocking; but I read a phrase about a year ago, an apparently simplistic little phrase, to the effect that there are just two activities. One is effective, and one isn't. Of course, it struck me as being dreadfully simplistic. And then I began to apply it to everything that human beings . . . every activity that a human being may find himself involved in. I discovered, in truth, there are only two courses to take. And that's certainly true in music. However sensitive a musician may be, if you don't find the means to express that sensitivity, express your view technically, you won't be able to project what you have to say to a third party. Therefore, the recording is extremely helpful; and I've found that, yes, it has affected my performances, but only to the good.

BADAL: Do you conduct differently for a recording than you do for a live concert?

MAAZEL: I don't draw a line between a recorded performance and a live performance. The only exception in this as far as I'm concerned is the area of timing, because there are certain spaces that cannot be filled aurally. The visual effect, obviously, is a component and should be, and should be. A dramatic sweep of the hand across a guitar means nothing except a lot of wrong notes and cut fingernails on a recording. And yet in the concert hall that rhetorical sweep of the hand is very important—very effective and important, extremely important. And when you realize that those effects, the visual effects, if you will—those which play a role in projecting your expression—cannot be used, then obviously your timing is affected, and you tend to tighten spaces between notes. Also, there is a question of the acoustics of the hall. Usually one records in halls with a great deal of resonance. One tends to adjust tempi, depending on the nature of the work, to that sound. But then one does so anyway in a live performance, and one should.

BADAL: In the ten years you've been conductor of the Cleveland Orchestra, the ensemble has made many recordings with you but few with other conductors. In that same time frame, the Chicago Symphony has recorded with five major conductors. Which arrangement is better for an orchestra?

MAAZEL: Well, I think that a major orchestra should record with several

conductors, providing they are major conductors. I would think, perhaps, three or four. But the Cleveland Orchestra was a very special case.
The Cleveland Orchestra had no recording program when I arrived here.
They were not considered to be commercial. And it was my task as music director to prove the contrary, that any orchestra enjoying a fine reputation could also enjoy that reputation while selling a lot of records. So it
was my task to establish the reputation of the orchestra again in the
recording field, which we managed to do over a period of five or six
years. And then the association of the orchestra with me became so firmly
planted in the minds of the record-buying public that other conductors
. . . it didn't seem likely they would record with the orchestra, even
though I would have welcomed that. That is not the situation now, however. Now as my tenure is coming to an end, I've gone out of my way to
see to it that other conductors record with the orchestra, take up the
slack. It will be recording with other conductors, and I think that's very
good.

BADAL: Can an orchestra establish a character of its own apart from a conductor?

MAAZEL: Yes, an orchestra can achieve, and every orchestra does, a kind of
character of its own. The conductor who knows his job, who is a fine
technician, who knows how to make an orchestra sound, can take a
student orchestra made up of good players and produce a performance
that would be as characteristic of his view as that recorded with the
Berlin Philharmonic or the Vienna Philharmonic. But there are orchestras, because of their tradition, their roots, which develop personalities
of their own, such as the Berlin Philharmonic, such as the Vienna Philharmonic. American orchestras with character? Yes! I think I would rec-
ognize the Cleveland Orchestra, though the orchestra has a much more
homogeneous sound. Very sensitive! A very versatile orchestra! It does
respond to what's demanded of it but will not necessarily give an idiom-
atic performance if there is not someone of great authority at the helm,
which is not the case with the Vienna Philharmonic or the Berlin Philharmonic. They will play idiomatically and well irrespective of who's
conducting; but the performance will be much, much better, a much
greater performance, if there's a good conductor there.

BADAL: You have stressed the importance of orchestras utilizing all forms of
media: recording, filmmaking, television. Yet European orchestras seem to
be much more involved in this sort of activity than American orchestras.

MAAZEL: One of the problems is money. The A. F. of M. [American Federation of Musicians] contract prohibited any work of this nature at all. In order to develop an idea, you need time, and the cost is so prohibitive as to nip any initiative in the bud. It's not just a matter of subsidy in Europe; it's just a different way of viewing the role that TV plays. Orchestras are paid and paid handsomely, but the contractual arrangements are such that you don't have to have up front money of several hundred thousand dollars to be paid within two weeks if you should want to record an orchestra, which is the case here. It's an immense amount of money. That contract has been renegotiated, as we all know, because the A. F. of M. has come to realize that it has prevented American orchestras from getting involved in what can be, in the long run, a very lucrative and artistically an extremely interesting affair.

BADAL: You have made many recordings with the Cleveland Orchestra. Why are works which you have performed with the orchestra, such as Tippett's *A Child of Our Time* and Britten's *War Requiem,* passed over?

MAAZEL: Well, again we're dealing with some facts of life. I don't know how many times I've attempted to get some of our contemporary music programs even funded, foundations, whatever! Get them on record. And just to no avail. And I do have a lot of clout. And I just . . . I wasn't able to swing it. There's one recording of the Britten.[1] Very lovely! I would have loved to have recorded that and made several attempts to get it recorded, just to no avail. You see, there was a crisis, a recording crisis, about three or four years ago. The market just fell apart. And there was a plethora of recordings and a dearth of sales. It was a bad situation. And of course, the digital, and in addition to the digital, the threat of the video disc! No one is taking any chances whatsoever. They're rerecording the basic repertoire inch by inch and watching the market very, very carefully. And it's going to be more Beethoven, more Brahms. I'll be recording a great deal for CBS. As you may know, I have a five-year contract with them, and that calls for something like fifty LPs. I also have a very long term and deep relationship with Deutsche Grammophon. I'll be working with them a great deal. So I may produce one hundred LPs in the next five years, almost all of which will be right in the center of the repertoire.

BADAL: Many record collectors would say that the sound quality on CBS is mediocre and the pressings are noisy. If this is the case, does it do you or the orchestra any good to appear on CBS?

MAAZEL: With regard to CBS, you're quite right. The pressings were not good. The quality of the recordings was very good, but the pressings here in the United States were poor because they were being pressed by people who knew nothing about classical music. There's been a profound reform at CBS in the last two years, and everything has changed at Masterworks. They've now bought a new laboratory for pressing; they've changed the administration profoundly. They're aware of the problem. It's no problem in Europe because the tapes, which were very good, were pressed in Europe.[2]

BADAL: Record companies are sometimes accused of exploiting promising talent before it has fully developed.

MAAZEL: They were at certain times. I think things have settled into place now. The companies have learned their lesson. They lost a fortune, mainly because people were incompetent. It takes a long time to become competent, very long. You can show a lot of promise, but if you have four hours to record a fifty-five-minute piece that's complex, you've got to have a lot of experience under your belt. And since each quarter of an hour costs $15,000, you can't waste time. You need accomplished, competent soloists who will go into the studio and do the job beautifully. And that takes a very high degree of professionalism. I've heard hundreds of broadcasts of artists I've never heard of who are very brilliant and who were working wherever—Phoenix, Calgary, New York. If someone is truly of value, he doesn't have to be nurtured by a recording company. He's just going to pop into public view because he deserves it. The era of the undiscovered talent is long since dead. It's not with us at all. We have too many discoveries of untalented people.

BADAL: Don't people tend to think of any artist in terms of what he has recorded?

MAAZEL: That I don't know. I've no way of knowing that. Some people like Michelangelo and Celibidache hardly record, and their careers are extraordinary. On the other hand, you have many artists who have recorded everything who are no better thought of today than they were many years ago; I can think of one conductor who I think has recorded every piece ever written. Their reputations haven't been helped or hurt. It's just they've recorded. Fine! Everybody takes note of it, but it doesn't mean anything insofar as their careers are concerned. A career is really a meshing of several undertakings, initiatives, one of which is recordings. Television plays a role too. All of these play a role.

BADAL: You are often given credit for being the first major conductor to make digital recordings. How did your association with Telarc come about, and what do you think of digital sound?

MAAZEL: Hearing in this case is believing. I was in Japan, and Mr. Akio Morita, a good friend of mine of the Sony Company, played a digitally recorded opera for me, which at that time was not in commerce. It was the first digital recording ever made. It was made alongside the analog. And I was absolutely stupefied. It was just incredible. And when the technique was explained to me, and I understood why the sound was so pristine and pure as it was. . . . And then when Telarc came along about six months later with a relationship with Soundsteam, they showed me what they could do, and I said, "Yes, that's great. Let's go ahead and do it."

This is the sound of the future; there's no questions about it. The difference is so, is so . . . . Many people don't realize they don't have the proper playback equipment for digital recording. In four or five years we're going to have it, and then everything that's being done today will come into its own. The difference today is, let's say, a 10 percent jump in quality, but when you hear it on digital playback equipment, you're in heaven. You really are in heaven because it's the purest sound. It's purer than the sound itself, if you know what I mean. Somehow hearing an instrument—there are visual interruptions. A lot of people listen to music with their eyes closed in a concert hall; but still there is the sound of a distant trolley, an overhead flight, or a radiator or something, or a creaking chair, somebody rustling a program, or a cough, or whatever. This is just pure sound. And to be in your room with a wraparound situation, then you're in heaven; you're in sound heaven.

Notes

1. At the time, the composer's own recording remained the only available version. There have been others since.

2. CBS is now Sony.

COLIN DAVIS

۶

ONE OF THE keys to a successful recording career is to find a niche. Colin Davis found his with a French composer on a Dutch label. After some sporadic studio activity early in his career for EMI and L'Oiseau-Lyre, Davis signed with Philips in the mid-sixties and began to record Berlioz.

The Colin Davis Berlioz cycle stands as one of the phonograph's most significant achievements. Well over a decade in the making, the series embraced virtually everything Berlioz wrote involving the orchestra, including the first commercial recordings of the operas *Benvenuto Cellini* and *Les Troyens*. A large measure of Davis's success with the French master derives from his ability to stress the delicate, even classical side of the composer's thinking as well as the romantically extravagant.

As his years with Philips coincided with his tenure at Covent Garden in London, Davis's discography includes a number of operas. Of these, his readings of Mozart, Britten, and Tippett tended to garner more favorable critical attention than his forays into Verdi and Puccini.

More recently he has recorded for Sony, RCA, and the relatively small German label Orfeo.

Our interview occurred at Severance Hall in March of 1982. Davis had made a spectacular debut with the Cleveland Orchestra the summer before at the Blossom Music Center, and the rumor mills were circulating his name freely as a possible successor to Lorin Maazel. At the time of the interview, Davis was fighting a crippling case of laryngitis, and the rigors of the morning rehearsal had clearly eroded his vocal resources. Still, he pressed on gamely—sometimes relaxing in his chair, sometimes slapping the closed score on the desk before him for emphasis—until by the end of the interview his voice had dwindled to little more than a hoarse whisper. ۶

Colin Davis. Author's collection.

BADAL: Maestro, the older generation of conductors, men like Toscanini and Furtwängler, hated records. They hated the physical process of making them, and they hated the results—not just because they sounded inadequate. I think they had an aesthetic objection to the whole idea of making a record. Now, someone like yourself who has made a lot of records, and a lot of very significant records, must have come to some kind of terms aesthetically with the whole idea of recording. Why do you think your point of view is different from theirs?

DAVIS: Well, they didn't have the same techniques as we do. They had to play six-minute sections to fit on one side of a 78, and if anything went wrong, they had to go back to the beginning and do it again. Then they had to stop, and then they had to do the next bit. That is really no way to make music, now is it? It's amazing the records came out as well as they did. Now we have a technique whereby we can play the whole piece through, and then if there are little disasters, we can patch them up.

BADAL: Would you call yourself an adherent to the long-take principle?

DAVIS: Oh, but of course. I mean, that's obvious. Sometimes one gets into the position when one is recording an opera of having to do it in all the wrong order, and it is amazing how it sounds, for the most part, logical. The musical mind has some means of kind of locking in where it should be.

BADAL: I suppose it would be easier to record a Mozart opera out of sequence than it would be Wagner, for example.

DAVIS: Yes, of course it would. That is certainly so. But I regard records principally as information. What has happened is that the whole of the musical literature as we have it from the sixteenth century onward is now available—or it was available, because, unfortunately, gramophone record companies are not primarily interested in music. They're interested in money, and if they don't make money, they tend to delete the music [from their catalog], which, of course, irritates musicians enormously. I wanted to get a recording of a certain Mozart string trio, and it was deleted. That's a scandal. I have a very small opinion of the musical commitment of record companies, and I'm sure they would entirely agree with me. But when one has made available, for example, all the chamber music of Schoenberg and Berg, and all the chamber music of Bach and Brahms, and so on, you've done something useful. And then if anyone wants to, he can go to a library, borrow a record, and find out what that music is like. I feel that I've done something useful with the recordings of the Berlioz pieces because they weren't available, and nobody really knew that music because nobody played it. Records are immensely useful now because opera houses always refer to them.

BADAL: So you're saying that records have a certain educational value.

DAVIS: It's information. It's actually there. And if you want to know what *Beatrice and Benedict* sounds like, you can go and get a record and find out, whereas before, you couldn't. If you looked the piece up in a book, somebody would say, "Oh well, Berlioz wasn't a very good composer anyway," and you would come away with no idea about the piece at all and probably no interest in it.

BADAL: I must say I never thought Berlioz was a good composer until I heard your recordings. I like the *Symphonie fantastique* as much as anybody, and I get a physical kick out of the massed parts of the Requiem, but I never really liked him until I heard your recordings.

DAVIS: Well then, perhaps I have been useful. But beyond that, I don't feel that making records is really a true way of making music, because there's nobody there to listen to it. It's a slightly incestuous thing because it's musicians making music with musicians, trying to produce something perfect, which is impossible because we are human, and we do make mistakes, and nothing that we do in a performance is that perfect—not perfect in that sense, in a scientific sense. The human element is variable, and very often the performance of a piece is greater than the number of mistakes that are made in it. That's one aspect of it. The other is that a record is really like a dead butterfly pinned to a wall in a museum. I much prefer to see them flying around.

BADAL: Do you listen to your own recordings?

DAVIS: Well, I listen to them when they come out because I want to know what kind of job we've made of it, and then I very rarely listen to them again—unless it's some particular piece, say, Sibelius's Sixth Symphony, which nobody plays, and I want to hear that particular sound. Actually, the last time I wanted to hear Sibelius's Sixth, it turned out to be Lorin Maazel and the Vienna Philharmonic, and that was lovely. But I won't listen to my recording of *Tosca* unless I have to conduct *Tosca*. I have, however, listened to the recording we made of the *Missa Solemnis,* more than once.[1] And although it is by no means a perfect recording, I think that is the thing of which I am most proud. I think that sounds, to me, something like Beethoven in his struggle with God.

BADAL: There was a time I thought the *Missa Solemnis* was the greatest piece of music ever written by anybody, and I'm not sure I don't still believe that.

DAVIS: As I said on the Marathon,[2] it is the greatest piece of public music. That leaves out things like the Mozart string quintets, so we don't have to get into that. But it is astounding, and I was proud of that recording.

BADAL: How do you use recordings? Simply, as you say, as information—to find out what a piece is like?

DAVIS: Yes. I mean, if I've got to do the Berg *Three Pieces for Orchestra* and I've never heard them, I can't see any shame in following a record and just getting an impression of the kind of sound. Of course, I'm lucky enough to have done *Wozzeck* and *Lulu,* so I know what to expect. And I don't think there's anything wrong in that. People say that if you listen to gramophone records too much, you'll become so used to the performance that all you'll do is imitate it. That is absolutely untrue. All that happens to me when I listen to a record is I see the possibilities; and since I don't want the piece to go that way, I can't bear to listen to it again. Even with my own recordings I think, gosh, that was ten years ago. That was absolutely dreadful.

BADAL: Is that why you rerecorded the *Symphonie fantastique?*

DAVIS: No. I rerecorded the *Symphonie fantastique* because the record company wanted me to. And so I did.[3]

BADAL: I've noticed that certain kinds of performances don't repeat well. You take a Furtwängler radio tape, for example. The first or second time you play it, you can be absolutely bowled over by the incredible intensity.

DAVIS: You never want to hear it again.

BADAL: You don't want to hear it too many times. The very qualities that make it so exciting the first few times don't repeat very well.

DAVIS: That's right.

BADAL: Your performances repeat very nicely.

DAVIS: I don't know that. I don't know that. But then I'm a certain kind of musician who does not go in for eccentricities—I hope. The man who doesn't is probably more bearable more often. But I don't leave out the eccentricities *because* I want people to listen to my records. That's not it at all. I just happen to be that kind of man, and that's my attitude toward it. Now, listening to music in a concert hall has nothing to do with listening to records. It's a different attitude altogether. First of all, someone is there playing; the orchestra is there playing. That's already exciting. And the people who have come have taken the trouble to shave and put some clothes on—they may be in blue jeans, but I'll bet they've washed—and they've made an effort. They've come expecting something.

The man who goes home, worn out, and puts on a disc is not in that frame of mind at all. When you're sitting in your own room listening, there's no adrenaline running. There's nothing at all except a desire to find pleasure, or, if you're a musician, a kind of clinical appraisal of what's going on. When I listen to tapes of live performances I've given, goodness me, I learn what I'm doing wrong. And that's why the Furtwängler performance isn't going to work on record. If the listener had been in a hall with the Berlin Philharmonic, he would have probably gone out blown out of his mind. But when you hear Furtwängler do a Brahms symphony, and he makes those special slowing downs which interrupt, for me, the logic of the performance, and he's not there doing it, I can't enjoy it. When I heard Toscanini's *Missa Solemnis* on record, I got in such a rage that he should do such a thing that I didn't even want to get to the end. Whereas if I had been there, I might have accepted it.

BADAL: Do you conduct differently for records than you do for a concert?

DAVIS: I'm trying to make music the way I want it to sound. I mean, that's all I can do. I'm just mad about music, and that's how it is. I'm trying to find the life of that music, whether it's for a recording or whether it's for the audience.

BADAL: There was a time when the range of interpretive possibilities seemed very great. Say Toscanini, Klemperer, Furtwängler, and Walter doing the Beethoven Fifth. That range seems to have narrowed. Differences between conductors today don't seem as great. Is that simply an evolution of musical understanding or are recordings playing a part, establishing interpretive boundaries which some people feel they can't go beyond?

DAVIS: I haven't the faintest idea about that. But since you ask the question, I'm going to put this to you. There has been an explosion of scholarship since the men you are mentioning were in their prime. There is much more attention given to the detailed instructions in the score. From what we read about Wagner's conducting and Mendelssohn's, and so on, they were pretty cavalier with the music they conducted. Wagner complained about Mendelssohn taking everything too fast. Wagner was famous for his accelerandi and his wild crescendos, and all the rest. Berlioz was famous for his clinical French mind, which didn't go in for those kind of excesses, though his music does sometimes. They certainly were much freer in their own subjective, romantic response to music. We have dropped all that really, and we try quite seriously to get back to what the composer could possibly have meant. We are less concerned with ourselves possibly, possibly. I'm not saying it's better or worse. There's no moral judgment in this. But it wasn't until the middle of the nineteenth century that anyone had heard of the *St. Matthew Passion*.

BADAL: Thanks to Mr. Mendelssohn.

DAVIS: Exactly, and what the devil they knew about John Wilbye or Purcell or Orlando Gibbons! And all those fantasies where there weren't any bar lines at all and the rhythm was completely free! Did they know anything about that at all? I doubt it. The editions of Mozart that you find in the nineteenth century are really not what we think of as Mozartian at all. And all these men you've mentioned were born in the nineteenth century and carried that tradition with them.

BADAL: With the passage of time, orchestras seem to have lost something of the distinctive characteristics they had forty or fifty years ago, with certain exceptions, such as the Vienna Philharmonic or some of the East German orchestras. But it seems to me that if you play recordings made in the twenties or thirties, you are much more conscious of—

DAVIS: National characteristics.

BADAL: I'm wondering if records have played a part in the disappearance of those national differences.

DAVIS: That I don't know. But I do know that it's Mahler and Bruckner who have changed all that. In Paris, they all played with vibrato, and they used to play their French bassoons, and their clarinets made a certain kind of noise. Then along came Solti and Barenboim wanting to play Bruckner and so on, and they demanded that they play German horns and buy Heckel bassoons. So they don't play with vibrato any more. It's a different thing. I went to the Orchestre de Paris, and we did Ravel. And I said, "What's happened? We should play it like Frenchmen. Play it with vibrato." They all laughed because that's gone. I loved it. It was beautiful what they used to do. But the first horn in Dresden plays with vibrato, and that surprised me no end. Very beautiful.

BADAL: You just made some recordings with the Dresden Staatskapelle.

DAVIS: That's a beautiful orchestra. So it's the kind of music that has become popular, especially with conductors, that has ironed out the sound. There are still national ways of playing the oboe, certainly, and the clarinet. There's the English clarinet. And the Berlin clarinet, which is a round sound. Then there's the Italian, which is very thin, and the French, which is thin. But it's strange that the Orchestre de Paris has an English-sounding clarinet player.

BADAL: So this might be a function of the jet age rather than records.

DAVIS: I think so.

BADAL: Record companies are sometimes accused of doing one of two things: on the one hand, they are often accused of ignoring new talent and concentrating on established names in established repertoire; on the other hand, they are sometimes accused of finding new talent and exploiting it before it is ready. Do you have any comment on this?

DAVIS: I have only one comment, and that is that the prime business of a recording company is to make money. Actually, they haven't got a hope in hell of making money, so all they're trying to do is lose as little as possible. They don't really have any artistic line of thought or development. And we have to face that. They may feel very affronted if I say that, but I know that this is true. I will not bore you with my experiences with my own record company—not that it's mine, but I've had a relationship with it for fifteen years. Sadly, I've come to that conclusion.

BADAL: From my perspective, were I a musician, I would far rather record for your company than a few others I could name.

DAVIS: Yes, that is probably true. Philips has a very good record in this respect.

BADAL: There was an interview that Bruno Walter gave when he was eighty. One thing he stressed was the historical aspect of records. A singer can play a Caruso record and hear where he took his breath. Or someone can hear how Toscanini phrased something. Is this important to you?

DAVIS: Oh, yes. That is the most positive aspect of it. We have now laid down fifty years of the history of musical performance. That's beautiful because you can fish out, if you want, Grumiaux's two old recordings of the Mozart violin concertos. I don't know if you can get them any more, but every kid who plays the fiddle should hear them, because there's something about the way Grumiaux played that fiddle which is unbelievable. Or if you can find the old recordings of Menuhin playing the Elgar! I was brought up on Kreisler's Beethoven Concerto and Mischa Elman's Tchaikovsky. And Schnabel playing the Beethoven G Major Concerto. I remember those things, and they were wonderful. There's something special about Rachmaninov and Kreisler playing Schubert's *Grand Duo.* These things should be preserved, and people should hear the way they played. You may not like it, but they were great musicians. What comes out of these people is that search for the life of the music.

It's a different kind of taste, but it's still genuine. Something else I want to stress is all the men you've mentioned learned their trade in the opera house. How many people are doing that now?

BADAL: Not too many. If I remember your biography, you did.

DAVIS: I'm still there. I think that's the place where you find out about conducting and find out about music, because all this wonderful symphonic music really began in the theater, and the theater really began in the church.

BADAL: Well, it's like drama too.

DAVIS: Well, it is, isn't it? How can you really handle a Bruckner symphony if you don't know *Die Meistersinger* or *The Ring?* Bruckner worshiped Wagner. He was his god. You can't approach it the other way around. And when you've done the fourteen hours of *The Ring,* a Mahler symphony doesn't seem so long.

BADAL: I read your negative comments on Mahler.

DAVIS: Yes, the Fifth is a bit of a problem for me; but really, some of his music is so wonderful, and I was only being a bit naughty because Mahler is such the fashionable composer now.

BADAL: Bruno Walter also said in that same interview that he was glad that all traces of his career as a performer would not disappear. Now, you're far from being an old man, and certainly nowhere near as old as he was when he made that statement, but do any such thoughts enter your mind as you're making a recording?

DAVIS: Not really, in that sense. I think I've done, as I say, some useful things. If I hadn't fought three battles, four battles, there wouldn't be any recordings of the Berlioz pieces. I took seven years—it's like Jacob and his wife, and then he got the wrong wife and had to work another seven—to get *The Trojans* on record, seven years. It took almost as long to get *Peter Grimes.* And then there was *The Midsummer Marriage* and all those Tippett pieces. If we hadn't done *The Midsummer Marriage,* nobody would know that music. I do feel that it's perhaps been useful. That doesn't count as a tremendous statement about anything. But I am pleased with certain things that we've done. I was very pleased with those Sibelius symphonies we made in Boston.

BADAL: What do you think about the debate between digital and analog sound?

DAVIS: I'm sorry, I don't find any of it interesting. I can't really tell if you play me a recording whether it's digital or not. I don't listen to music like that. I'm not a hi-fi fiend. All I'm doing is listening to the music itself, so I really don't know. It's like playing Mozart to cows so they give more milk. Let's try them with digital! If it turns into butter, there must be something wrong.

The only thing I can say about the new technology is that records will have to be made all over again, and people will have to buy an awful lot more equipment. The industry, you know, is in grave difficulties because the whole literature has been recorded. There is hardly a work by Dittersdorf that you can't get somewhere or other. And this is the tragedy of our civilization. Our literature has come to an end, and it's wearing out. There is, of course, all the experimental music, but we shall not live long enough to know whether Stockhausen's *Donnerstag* or Boulez's *Eclats* will be the daily fare fifty or one hundred years from now. Berlioz said, "One hundred years from now people will listen to my music," and he was right. And Mozart! He didn't say that, but he's there too. He came out right on top of all of them, that poor little man. For the moment, the great tradition of Europe has come to an end with its last daughter, which is music. And I happen to feel that it is our duty to preserve this thing because it's the only thing we've got left.

BADAL: Ingmar Bergman said something very similar.

DAVIS: Well, I think many of us feel this. And that is why music is so important to us and why we must not do it any harm.

Notes

1. The reference here is to his Philips recording. He has since produced a digital version on RCA.

2. The annual WCLV-FM Marathon to raise money for the Cleveland Orchestra.

3. This refers to his second recording of the piece with the Concertgebouw Orchestra of Amsterdam. His earlier recording was with the London Symphony. He later made a digital version with the Vienna Philharmonic. All three were for Philips.

KURT MASUR

꜡

ONE OF THE positive aspects to working as a performing musician in communist East Germany was that artists with the state-supported VEB Deutsche Schallplatten could record almost anything they wished without having to keep a vigilant eye on the bottom line. Though the regime's inherent conservatism placed any radically modern musical experimentation off limits, Kurt Masur was able to record, along with the expected standard repertoire items, some major projects of undoubted value during his long and continuing tenure with the venerable Leipzig Gewandhaus: a massive Liszt cycle, including all the tone poems, the oratorios, and the music for piano and orchestra; Schumann's virtually unknown opera *Genoveva*; and a multidisc exploration of Max Bruch's music for violin and orchestra.

When Germany was still divided, segments from Masur's vast discography were licensed for released in the West through EMI, Philips, Teldec, and Eurodisc. Since the fall of the Berlin Wall and his appointment to the New York Philharmonic, Masur has continued his association, or forged more direct ties, with most of these labels.

I interviewed Kurt Masur in July of 1982, when he conducted the Cleveland Orchestra at Blossom. His comment about music banned by the Nazis is interesting since no one else has recorded as much Mendelssohn as he: all the early string symphonies, two cycles of the canonical five symphonies, both oratorios *St. Paul* and *Elijah, Die erste Walpurgisnacht,* the piano concerti, the Violin Concerto, and the incidental music to *A Midsummer Night's Dream.* The possible second cycle of Beethoven symphonies to which he briefly refers finally appeared in 1993 on Philips—the first recordings based on the new critical editions of the scores published by C. F. Peters. His stated desire to record a Prokofiev series and the complete symphonies of Shostakovich has so far not been realized. ꜡

Kurt Masur in rehearsal with the New York Philharmonic. Photo by Chris Lee. Courtesy of the New York Philharmonic.

BADAL: Maestro, you've only been in Cleveland once before; and yet, if you were to talk with local music lovers, they would probably know your name. And I think that's because you've made so many records. Do you have any thoughts about records as an aid to building your career or, in the case of your orchestra the Leipzig Gewandhaus, to making it better known in the West?

MASUR: I must tell you one thing. Normally I'm not the type to think of building a career. I have only tried to be a good musician, and I am always happy if people understand what I want to tell them, what I think about and what I feel about these works I am conducting. For my orchestra, it's another case, and in that case, you are right. Recordings help a lot. You can say the same thing about the Cleveland Orchestra. Cleveland is a beautiful city, one of the most beautiful places on Lake Erie, but Cleveland is not a city in the center of the world. But I think for America, for the United States, your orchestra has the richest tradition you can think of. Of course, I know that the New York Philharmonic is your oldest orchestra; but the Cleveland Orchestra under George Szell and continuing with Maazel makes—

BADAL: And now with Dohnányi!

MASUR: And Dohnányi, of course, a very old, good friend of mine—makes a part of the history of the United States, and I think a very important part. And recordings help make the orchestra better known.

BADAL: Maestro, you are young enough to have grown up with recordings available to you. Did recorded music play any role in your formative musical education?

MASUR: The radio did, yes! When I was young, I listened very often to the radio, and I must tell you, a few of the impressions I received I have never forgotten in my whole life. I heard Bruno Walter's first performance after the Second World War with Mozart's G Minor Symphony. It must have been 1946. As I understand, he was in West Berlin, I think. And this was one of the deepest impressions I ever received. And so I started to try to find out what kind of person he was. Really, he led me on my way even though I never could meet him. And then also at the same time, there were very often transmissions from the open rehearsals of the Boston Symphony under Charles Munch. They came over the radio in West Germany, mostly for the American forces network. And this was also very inspiring for me, because they played a lot of pieces we could never hear in the Nazi time, and this was another impression I received.

BADAL: You know, you mention Bruno Walter. When he was eighty years old, he was interviewed, and the subject of recordings came up. He said one of the most important things about recordings was the historical aspect. Do you consider the historical aspect of recordings very important?

MASUR: I think in one way, yes! You can listen to a lot of recordings and can compare them with your own ideas about a work. And if you find a way, if you think, "Oh, that's it! This is what I was always looking for, to do this like that. I wanted to have the sound like this," then you can learn a lot. But I must tell you, I always avoid hearing records just before I am conducting a piece. There are a lot of young conductors who are trying to copy great conductors, and they are starting not to be creative by themselves. And that's a danger. There was a time when recordings were not so dominating, when perfection was not so dominating. Only making music. And then the spirit of the music and the mentality of the artist came out. Then you can learn a lot about interpretation.

BADAL: Do you think the proliferation of recordings is destroying the spirituality of music? Is there too much pursuit of perfection?

MASUR: There was more danger of this ten or fifteen years ago, when perfection was more dominating. Now you can notice that a lot of music lovers are buying the recordings of Bruno Walter, of Toscanini, of Furtwängler, of the old conductors, of the old pianists, of the old singers, because they feel there is something here which they haven't had.

BADAL: What do you think is the greatest benefit recordings have?

MASUR: The greatest importance of recordings is that anybody who wants to can play at home, at any time, a piece which he likes.

BADAL: Something which I just finished playing last night, and speaking of Bruno Walter again, was Hans Pfitzner's *Palestrina,* which is almost never performed in this country. Bruno Walter conducted the world premiere in 1917, and the last letter he wrote in his life was to Frau Pfitzner. In that letter he said that he thought *Palestrina* would survive, that it had all the elements of greatness. And I thought, I would never have been able to hear that work if it weren't for recordings.

MASUR: Yes, and we are very proud that we did the first recording of Schumann's *Genoveva.* The opera! This is the same. And I think television is also very important. You can send to anybody up in the hills who is never able to come down to any city a concert, a great performance. He can listen. He can take part. And this is a wonderful thing in our time.

BADAL: The world community of musical understanding.

MASUR: Yes, I think so.

BADAL: Let me get just a little philosophical. Music is an art that exists in time. And if you were to conduct the same piece twice in a row, the second performance would be different than the first. But the recorded performance is always going to be the same. And I know there are some musicians who are upset by that. Does that ever bother you?

MASUR: That's not a very nice feeling for an artist. As you know, you make a recording, and before it comes out to the audience, you are really one step beyond it. And you always get one of your recordings, listen to it and think, "Oh my God! What did I do?" And I think for instrumentalists, in a different way, it's even worse. I remember I had with David Oistrakh a talk as he started to conduct. He said to me, "Dear Masur! I know I will not be a great conductor. I only try to be as good a musician as I can be. But as a violinist, I can never play better than I did on recordings." I think, though, that everyone tries to go his own way. There are some good results. As you know, Karajan now is in the position to say, "I want to do this piece again, now!" And he does. But this is unique. Maybe

Solti can do something like this, too, but not more than three or four conductors can. But I was very glad that in the opening of our new Gewandhaus we could make the Ninth Symphony again, because, really, now it sounds so different from ten years ago.

BADAL: The Beethoven Ninth?

MASUR: Beethoven Ninth, yes.

BADAL: Are you going to do all the Beethoven symphonies again?

MASUR: Maybe yes! We have to start now because of digital recordings. And I think this opportunity gives you the possibility to show the audience that you are growing up, and maybe people understand better what you are trying to do.

BADAL: What do you feel are the greatest problems with recordings?

MASUR: Look, we talk about the recording always being the same. If you have a recording which is really perfect, you can play it again and again, but you feel the spirit doesn't change. It is not so painful for the listener as for the artist himself. But if you have any faults on the recording, then it is painful for the listener. You discover, "Oh, this is not together, and this was not together, and this was not so perfect." And then it starts to disturb you more and more because you expect it. And I think it is difficult to do a performance on records which is alive and perfect at the same time. I always tell my orchestra it is not enough to be perfect on recordings. It must be like a live performance which will bring people up from their seats.

BADAL: On a recording?

MASUR: Yes, on a recording.

BADAL: Do you find it difficult to work in the studio?

MASUR: No! No! I think we have a very good situation. If a recording is not finished, we continue it later. It's not a question of money and time. If we find out that we are not able to do a piece very well, so let's go, and next time we come together, try it again.

BADAL: Do you like the principle of the long take?

MASUR: I like it. I like it very, very much. Recording can make an orchestra very, very dead, and yourself also. So let the music go! And then very often we repeat small places, only to make . . . to repair it. Nothing else.

BADAL: As you look back at the recordings you have made, which ones are you the most proud of?

MASUR: I must tell you, I think I'm always in the kind of mood in which I would tell you I want to do it again and better. I never will be proud of a single result. I'm proud that, with my orchestra, we could grow, working together with a recording company. And that's a result I'm proud of, but that's a result of twelve years.

BADAL: Are there some things you would like to record that you haven't had the chance to record yet?

MASUR: Yes. We ended with Liszt. We are now starting the whole works of Prokofiev. And then we will start the whole symphonies, and maybe the whole works, of Tchaikovsky. And then I would like to do all the symphonies of Shostakovich because I was a very close friend to him. And I think the Gewandhaus was the only orchestra in the world which did a cycle of his symphonies within two seasons. He was very glad about it.

BADAL: Do you like making recordings? Do you like the process?

MASUR: I don't hate it. I don't hate it. I must tell you that if I am able to concentrate on the work as I would in a concert, the microphones don't disturb me. They are not disturbing to me.

BADAL: Why do you suppose the older generation of conductors hated making records so much? I mean men like Toscanini, Furtwängler, Klemperer, Walter. You know, they hated the process, and they hated the results.

MASUR: Of course. Because they had the feeling that their concerts were much more perfect than they were. It is a very, very true story that Furtwängler, as he listened to his first recordings, went away and was not able to listen anymore because he found them so bad. It wasn't together. It was not perfect. It was not in the right tempo. So he discovered his own faults. It was a bad surprise. But our generation now knows this about listening to our own recordings, and we expect it. And I think also that orchestras are better trained today, a little bit more perfect than the orchestras before.

BADAL: Let me ask you a question about orchestras. Thirty or forty years ago, orchestras seemed to have very different national characteristics. This doesn't seem to be quite so true anymore, with the exception of the Vienna Philharmonic and the Leipzig Gewandhaus. Do you think recordings have had anything to do with that?

MASUR: I don't think so. There is a different danger. Of course, if you would like to have the best musicians of the world and you have enough money to pay anybody. You start to build an orchestra, and somebody is coming from China, some from Japan, some from Germany, and so. You can build a fantastic orchestra, but this will be an international sound. You will never have the kind of individual profile, the special sound! And the secret of these old, traditional European orchestras is that they have their own schools. So Mendelssohn founded, more than 130 years ago, the high school for music in Leipzig. And still we get our members—more than 85 percent of our members in the Gewandhaus Orchestra are from this school. And it is not only the bad points—as Gustav Mahler said, "Schlamperei ist die Tradition"—but it is also, for our time, a kind of stability, of steadiness in an orchestra because you can feel this special old, traditional, maybe old-fashioned sound. And I think one should listen to these few orchestras because they are important in finding out what kind of sound Brahms must have, and Bruckner!

BADAL: Because of this traditional sound in an orchestra like the Leipzig Gewandhaus, would you be reluctant to record something like a Verdi opera?

MASUR: I would try to avoid it, yes. Of course, generally the orchestra plays everything. We also did a recording of works of Gershwin.

BADAL: I didn't know that.

MASUR: Yes, yes, we did. And we enjoyed it very much. I think it is not so bad, but still you hear the sound of the Gewandhaus. And our orchestra plays every evening at the opera, also Verdi. But it's another sound. It's another style. It's the Gewandhaus style.

BADAL: Do you listen to records?

MASUR: I do listen to records. But I must tell you one thing. I listen only to two kinds of records: very strange ones, jokes about classical music.

BADAL: The Hoffnung Festival?

MASUR: Hoffnung, yes. I like them. I have a lot of the Portmouth Symphony. I don't know if you know it. This is the kind of happening that I sometimes like very much. On the other hand, I listen to records of traditional—the recordings of Arthur Nikisch. I have a lot of the recordings of Furtwängler, of Bruno Walter, of Toscanini. And I always try to compare their styles and to find out why they went to this style. Because Toscanini's Brahms is so different from Bruno Walter's, and Bruno Walter's Brahms with American orchestras is different than with the Vienna Philharmonic Orchestra. This is very interesting for me. These records I listen to very much.

BADAL: What do you think of digital sound? Do you like it?

MASUR: Yes and no! I think we are still on the way with digital sound. I think it is at the moment a little bit dangerous to have this presence of sound, this kind of direct sound, naked sound, which makes a listener hear things he could never hear in the hall.

BADAL: Erich Leinsdorf tells a story in his book *The Composer's Advocate* about a man who listens to a lot of records, goes to a live concert, and doesn't like it because it doesn't sound like his stereo.

MASUR: Yes, yes, he's absolutely right. And I try in our recordings, together with the technical members of the crew, to avoid giving people a different kind of sound than they could expect in a concert hall.

BADAL: But still a good sound.

MASUR: Still a good sound. But still we try to bring out things which are not well heard in a concert hall. But I always tell any technical man, "Please, I want to hear on record what I am hearing when I stand in front of the orchestra."

BADAL: Do you see danger with the increased application of technology to music?

MASUR: If somebody tells me, "Close your eyes," and the sound from a stereo is as natural as that you could imagine if someone were in front of you making music, then I say that's the highest point we can reach. But very often you have a stereo set which makes a sound you never can hear from any instrument, you never can hear in any hall. And that's a danger, especially for our young people. They go into a disco, and they are used to hearing this sound. And then they are coming in to hear the—

BADAL: Electronic sound.

MASUR: Electronic sound! And then they are coming to hear the *Bolero* of Ravel and it is not disturbing for them because it is not enough. It is not enough. If I am at home, I like to play chamber music. I like to play very often on a clavichord. The sound is so small and so nice, and I have to listen very carefully so I can hear. And I always try to get to a point where I am able to hear whispering. If I am at home and I am listening to a fantastic stereo, maybe not only stereo but quadraphonic sound, and my ears are full of sound, it may be I feel like I have taken a wonderful drug, and I am very high. But if I am high, I am losing control, and I never will have a spiritual impression. And that's a danger because I think music is the kind of art which is able to fill your body, your heart, your soul, and your spirit.

ANTAL DORÁTI

⟋⟍

IN HIS AUTOBIOGRAPHY *Notes of Seven Decades,* Antal Doráti dismisses the often repeated assertion that he is the world's most recorded conductor as a typical bit of exaggerated public relations. Though Karajan and Bernstein probably surpass him in sheer numbers of discs, Doráti has indeed left a recorded legacy that remains impressive in size and scope.

During the fifties and sixties, the bulk of his recordings appeared in the United States on Mercury; in the seventies, he shifted most of his studio activity over to the London label, for which he produced such noteworthy items as the complete orchestral music of Kodály with the Philharmonia Hungarica and all the Tchaikovsky tone poems with the National Symphony Orchestra of Washington, D.C. As music director of the Detroit Symphony, he performed and recorded Richard Strauss's rarely heard *Die Ägyptische Helena.* Though a flawed performance of a seriously flawed opera, the set remains a souvenir of historical and sentimental value since Doráti had served as Fritz Busch's assistant at the work's 1928 Dresden premiere.

Of all the recordings Doráti made throughout his long career, however, none approach the significiance of his Haydn project, a massive undertaking, split between London and Philips, that occupied him for well over a decade. He had to peddle his plan to record all the symphonies to two other labels before London agreed to the huge, financially risky undertaking. When the three-year project reached completion in 1973, it sparked a virtual renaissance of interest in the little-known early Haydn symphonies among other labels and conductors. Unfortunately, the equally significant and superlatively performed series of operas for Philips ground to a halt after eight works: approximately half, including the marionette operas, of Haydn's surviving output for the stage.

For a while it looked as if my interview with Doráti would not take place. Appearing with the Cleveland Orchestra in September 1982, Doráti failed to show up in the conductor's office in Severance Hall at the appointed time, nor was he anywhere else in the building. Suddenly he strode vigorously into the office, flashed a magnificent smile, and apologized for his tardiness, explaining that he had taken advantage of the beautiful fall day and gone for a morning walk. ᵔ

Antal Doráti. Photo by Peter Hastings

BADAL: Maestro, of all the recordings you have made in your career, I suppose most collectors would associate you with that monumental project of all the Haydn symphonies. Did that take a lot of preparation on your part?

DORÁTI: Oh, yes. Because I didn't record these symphonies, for instance, as Haydn wrote them, one after the other—just waiting until God gave him an idea and then just writing it down. I had to do them upside-down and every which way. We started with the Symphony No. 56. That was the first one I put on tape. I had to be absolutely clear in my mind where that symphony belongs in the big scheme—what went before, what came after. To record the Beethoven nine symphonies, of course, is a wonderful thing. But every one of us grew up with them from our very childhood. If we record the Sixth, we very well know how it fits in between the First and the Ninth. But with these hundred . . . . There's actually material for 110 symphonies in this set, with all the extra movements and all the variants of symphonies. Now then, how else can one go about it except to make a tremendous study of the whole thing?

BADAL: But you actually planned, as I remember, how many sessions would be involved, how long each one would take.

DORÁTI: Approximately! We know the sessions in Europe are three hours. They are all three hours.

BADAL: Did you feel it was necessary to make this kind of preparation before you approached a record company?

DORÁTI: Yes, absolutely. Because the plan was so big that if they had been confronted with this rock, let us say, this block of marble, they would have been scared of it. And so I had to make a statue from the marble first and show them. "Here it is, that's what we want!"

BADAL: You said in your book that Decca was the third company you had approached.[1]

DORÁTI: Second. I think so. The book is correct; I don't remember.

BADAL: I'm just curious what kind of reasons the first companies gave for not going ahead with the project.

DORÁTI: Too big! Too complicated! No sales! Not popular enough.

BADAL: Good old-fashioned commercialism.

DORÁTI: That's right, that's right.

BADAL: Maestro, the fact that you would devote that much time and energy to such an incredibly massive project says to me that you really must believe recordings have a great deal of value.

DORÁTI: Recordings have a great deal of value, indeed yes. But not primarily in the sense which most people believe. What is important is that it is set down that in the seventies the Beethoven symphonies, by the finest artists of the epoch and the finest orchestras, were played like this. Beethoven's piano sonatas by the finest pianists of that decade, were played like this.

BADAL: So you would stress the historical importance of recordings?

DORÁTI: Yes! And also important is that less famous works be recorded, you know. The word "record" has two meanings. It means the disc which turns, and it means the record like of a marriage or a birth. Actually, the score of a piece is rather dead material. It is only good for us musicians, and we have to revive it. Whereas the sounding record is a living document of the result of the score. And I think it is important that records are there for general use. The fact that in your public library in Cleveland there are the complete works of Shakespeare is not important because other writers and other dramatists can see how Shakespeare wrote his plays; it is important because they are there, and everyone can see how Shakespeare wrote. Everyone can! And it will be very interesting to see how—already it is interesting to see how the same piece was played fifty years ago. And some of these records are good; some of them are impossible. I have heard performances on record which today are being rejected, and justly so. But at that time they were justified, and they were the best.

BADAL: Maestro, the generation of conductors to which you belong was really the first one to embrace recording. The generation before had their doubts about recordings. They hated the process, and they hated the results. What do you think happened to bring about this change of attitude?

DORÁTI: The only things which really count are the advent of the long-playing record and the advent of tape. You know, it was really hateful to have only four-and-a-half minutes of music, and then you had to stop, and then start again for the next segment, you know. And it was very difficult to give any continuity to a longer piece, a two-hour piece. And then, of course, the record was a rarity. It was not the rampant thing as it is now.

BADAL: Music is an art that exists in time. If you were to conduct the same piece twice in a row, the performances would be different.

DORÁTI: And that's what makes it a great art. And there I point out the great danger of records. The danger of the record is that it catches a moment's expression and eternalizes it in a way which shouldn't be. It is like a photograph which catches a person in a moment, and if you don't know that person, then that moment is a false impression. In an aphorism you could say that an immovable smile is a grimace.

BADAL: One of the books on Mahler that is currently available has a picture of him smiling. You don't usually see photographs of Mahler smiling, and it was a picture like it that his daughter once picked as the one that looked the most like him. She said, "This is the man that I remember."

DORÁTI: Yes, but she had, of course, the advantage, we might say, of knowing many of his faces. If someone only knew Mahler from that smile, he might think, "That's a hydrocephalic, that's a stupid man," you know. I went through this. I once went to visit a country in the New World, in South America. It was Colombia, where the orchestral culture was very, very little. Nevertheless, I went there, and I conducted. It was very interesting. I was a young man, and it was a very interesting experience. And I met music lovers in the country. These were mostly refugees from Europe, from the Hitlerian regime. And they were very, very poor. Nevertheless, they liked their music, and they liked to listen to it. They had records, and they made a record club. Then they came together and gave themselves recorded concerts twice a week or so. But they didn't have duplicates; they had only one recording of each work. I visited them, I talked to them. I found, to my horror, that they didn't know the music; they knew one interpretation, one rendition of that music—one rendition of the music, not the music itself. And what is interesting in music is that it is performed in several ways. I suppose it starts when a composer performs his music, his own work. He ceases to be a composer and becomes a performer with the same rights and same duties as any other performer. Naturally, he will always change. There will be no two performances alike. Even if we are convinced of a piece and should want him to make his performances alike, he will never succeed one hundred percent.

BADAL: You can tell this with musicians who have recorded the same piece more than once. There are tremendous differences sometimes.

DORÁTI: Oh yes, oh yes! Sometimes these changes are justified. Sometimes they are just whims. These, then, are not to be justified, these are not to be condoned. But if it is an evolution of penetration into the work's spirit, then it is justified; and if it is an evolution of one's own personality, then that's also justified. Here we come to the eternal question: how much should a performer inject his own person into the work he performs? A silly question! Because he cannot help but inject himself. The question should be asked this way: how much can the performer inject of the creator's intention? And he should try to inject the most, because his person, small man that he is, or woman, is an element he cannot eliminate. I should love to be Beethoven if I conduct the Symphony No. 7. But I never . . . . So even with my greatest ability, if I could have one iota of Beethoven's spirit, then already that's something. If I could have two moments of Beethoven's own spirit, it's much better. If I could have three, well . . . .

BADAL: There are people who would say that it is much easier to project that spirit during a concert than when you are making a recording.

DORÁTI: No, I would not say that it is so. But it requires a different philosophy, a different approach. When I am at a concert, I put my physical presence into the battle, so to say. It's not a battle, but I put my being there. Willy-nilly, my presence will exert some influence upon the hearer. Because I exert some influence on my colleagues, the performers, evidently it's something which gets to the hearer also. Although one should never try. That's another chapter of the conductor's life which we will have to have another interview for. So when I make a record, I am in fact obliged to make an extra effort to get even closer to the composer because when the record is played, I won't be there. Not only will the composer himself be absent, but I'll be absent as well.

BADAL: Anyone who listens to a lot of records very quickly learns that certain kinds of performances don't repeat well. My favorite examples are tapes of live Furtwängler performances. The first time you hear them, they are the most exciting things you can imagine. But the qualities that make them so exciting don't seem to repeat well.

DORÁTI: I believe you. Of course, I can't say. I haven't had the same experience. I have never had such experiences because I listen to very few records. I simply haven't got the time to listen to many records. But there are those personal things which are ephemeral, which are fleeting. Art altogether is a free expression of human beings, and there are no rules. I can't say what is the right way of making art. It's everybody's . . . matter of his own conscience between himself and his God.

BADAL: You say in your book that you made your first recordings in 1936.

DORÁTI: Something like that, yes.

BADAL: Do you remember the sessions at all?

DORÁTI: Oh, yes, very well.

BADAL: Do you remember what you recorded?

DORÁTI: Oh, yes. It was all ballet music which the Ballets Russes de Monte Carlo played at Covent Garden. And it was the London Philharmonic Orchestra. We went from the performances into the recording studio. It was *Le Beau Danube* by Johann Strauss. It was the *Sheherazade* by Rimsky-Korsakov. Of course, it was not ballet music; but it was danced to. It was *Jeux d'enfants* by Bizet. It was the *Polovetsian Dances* by Borodin. It was Stravinsky's *Baiser de la Fée*.

BADAL: All of that in those first sessions?

DORÁTI: Well, I'm telling you. We took as many sessions as were needed. Those were the first records, those half-dozen records.

BADAL: Do you like to make records? You've made so many.

DORÁTI: Oh, yes, yes! The quantity of my recordings shows that I enjoy it. Because if it were a tremendous sacrifice, then I wouldn't do it.

BADAL: What do you think of digital technology, Maestro?

DORÁTI: Well, recording began with the very primitive invention of Edison's, as you know. And I know you've heard how scratchy they sound. Then they made it somewhat better. Then records really sounded like music or speech. Then they made them even better. The humming was there, but not so much. Then came the long-playing record, which was a great advance. Now comes the digital record, which is even better. Now comes the compact disc which has made its appearance. I haven't heard them yet, but on my next appearance in Amsterdam the company promised to show them to me. So I will hear them then. This is almost like real music.

BADAL: All these developments in recording technology that you've mentioned took place during your lifetime, except, of course, the invention of recording itself.

DORÁTI: Yes, that was earlier. Indeed, I began with the 78s.

BADAL: Media theorists say that people tend to accept the level of technology they are born into but tend to regard further development as a danger.

DORÁTI: Not us who record! Certainly not the artists who participate in recordings.

BADAL: You've made so many records, and I saw that Beethoven series you made with the Detroit Symphony for PBS. So you are obviously comfortable with all the various technologies. Do you see any danger to music from the increased application of all this technology?

DORÁTI: Oh, no, I don't see any danger at all. I think it serves music. However, everything, you know, has a backwash. To everything there are disadvantages. Now, you could argue that while this tremendous mass of new listeners who are arriving to our kind of fine music is an advantage, the superficial knowledge of this music is some kind of danger.

BADAL: The sort of thing you mentioned earlier about only knowing one rendition of a piece rather than the music itself.

DORÁTI: That, I would say, is a danger, but it is a danger I would willingly undertake for the ultimate gain. It is the same thing as with the discovery of America. Don't you think that was a danger to discover all this new territory?

BADAL: Sure!

DORÁTI: Well, and aren't you happy that someone faced that danger?

BADAL: I'm glad they did, yes. What do you think are the *benefits* to music from recordings?

DORÁTI: There are two benefits. And I do not say that recording is a blessing. No! And I do not go on my knees to thank God that recording has arrived. No! Music would be just as interesting, beautiful, and deep without recordings. But here they are, here we have them, and they have advantages. The advantages are twofold: there are more people listening to music than before, and there are documents. I'm using "record" now in the other sense. There are documents of sounding music—not only printed music, not only music which is written down. Those are the two advantages.

BADAL: We can hear the repertoire that has been put on records.

DORÁTI: Actually, yes. Before recording you could go into a library, a public library, and there are all the scores. These were of value to only a select minority, namely very good musicians who could read all this stuff. Now you can go into a public library, a record library, and get everything from Vivaldi to Penderecki and listen with your own ears without having to learn anything.

Note

1. *Notes of Seven Decades,* rev. ed. (Detroit: Wayne State University Press, 1981).

ERICH LEINSDORF

ↄ

In one sense, Erich Leinsdorf had a rather strange career in the recording studios. During the 1950s, 1960s, and into the 1970s, he recorded frequently, building up a discography impressive in both size and diversity. He was virtually the house opera conductor for RCA and recorded a full complement of standard repertoire items by Wagner, Strauss, Mozart, Verdi, Puccini, and (rare for an Austrian-born conductor) Rossini, as well as novelties such as Korngold's *Die tote Stadt*. As music director of the Boston Symphony from 1962 to 1969, he recorded not only such standard fare as Beethoven and Brahms symphony cycles but works by Berg and Ginastera. And then suddenly—around the turn of the decade between the seventies and eighties—the entire industry seemed to lose interest in him, and one of the most prolific voices in the studio fell silent, though he remained very active in the concert hall.

Leinsdorf had been music director of the Cleveland Orchestra for a brief period in the mid-1940s, and after Maazel's departure he appeared regularly with the ensemble to provide a sense of continuity until Dohnányi's arrival. Our interview took place in November 1982 following a morning rehearsal. Things must have gone well, for the talkative maestro was clearly in a relaxed and jovial mood. Brandishing a cigar of true Churchillian majesty, he veered from combativeness to thoughtful reflection, from good-humored commentary to rigorously learned analysis, with awesome dexterity. ↄ

Badal: Do you remember your first recording session?
Leinsdorf: Vaguely! I think the first time I recorded was as a piano accompanist for a singer who sang Hugo Wolf songs. But I cannot with assurance pinpoint—it must have been in the middle 1930s.
Badal: When you made those first recordings, Maestro, what sort of role did recordings play in people's lives?

Erich Leinsdorf in rehearsal with the Cleveland Orchestra. Photo by Peter Hastings.

LEINSDORF: It was a wondrous thing. In Vienna we had a public place where there is now a very elegant sort of food department store, and there was a salon with booths where you could go and listen to recordings. They were like the machines which you have today in bars where people put coins into—

BADAL: Jukebox.

LEINSDORF: Jukeboxes, yes! And there was an entire repertoire of platters of whatever they had, and for the money you put in, you selected what you wanted to hear. I would say that the major attractions were the great singers with arias and Lieder. That is certainly the way I got familiar with the great singers: by going to this salon and listening to their voices.

BADAL: You know, in both your books *Cadenza* and *The Composer's Advocate,*[1] one of which I read with a great deal of pleasure and the other with a great deal of interest—

LEINSDORF: Thank you.

BADAL: —you speak about records and recording companies, and some-times rather harshly. And yet there are few conductors who have made as many records as you have. And so would it be safe to assume that, in spite of the difficulties inherent in the medium, you think recordings have value?

LEINSDORF: Recordings have enormous value; and it's very good of you to ask me these questions, because one can never be explicit enough. I think recordings are an almost unmitigated blessing for the public, for the music lover, but they have been abused by the professional. And my caution against using records for study is, of course, the basis of my second book which you so kindly mentioned before. I believe that the professional—the performer—be it a pianist or a conductor or a guitarist or whatnot—should study with the composer from the score and not with other performers from recordings. If a person . . . What I am telling you now is an improvised comparison which is not a good one.

BADAL: Sometimes improvisations work the best.

LEINSDORF: Well, let's see if it sits as any kind of good comparison. I, as a reader and layman of the literary world, read book reviews with the greatest of pleasure. I have several subscriptions to book reviews. Since one can't read all books, one might as well read the reviews of the important books which interest one. If I were a book reviewer, I should not read other reviews before reviewing a book myself. Because the critic, the book critic, should interpret a book for the person who reads the review. So if I want to interpret a book, I should not read another person's interpretation of the book. I should read the book myself and then write my review.

BADAL: What you are saying then is that one of the great dangers for a young musician with recordings is that the urge is going to be to imitate what he hears on a recording and not look closely at the score.

LEINSDORF: Or be hell-bent to do the opposite! And you cannot hear everything on recordings. You miss things. And you don't know under what circumstances records have been made. There have been many re-cordings which were issued, even from the most independent recording artists, which should never have been issued.

BADAL: I think I have some of those in my collection.

LEINSDORF: I'm sure! We all do. We all do. And I know how it goes. There are pressures brought to bear which of course one never admits publicly. But there are pressures, and one sometimes OK's something that one shouldn't have OK'd. So for all these reasons, technical and philosophical! But the main reason is it should not be another interpreter who leads a young conductor to the composer, whoever the composer is. My discontent with the record companies is centered around one single issue: that the major companies are unwilling, and have always been unwilling no matter if they were in prosperity or in distress, to record a work for the first time.

BADAL: I remember the difficulty you said you had in recording Mozart and Haydn with the Boston Symphony.

LEINSDORF: That was a matter of the master contract between the association and the union. That is a different thing, and that I really cannot charge to the record companies. That is a matter of collective bargaining which has never been successfully resolved with respect to the big orchestras, and that I certainly cannot charge against any record company. What I charge them with is this: lack of confidence in doing something for the first time. And there I have a very nice story. There was in Austria some sort of a decrepit aristocrat, Count Bobbie, of whom many stories are told. And one day a man comes to him and says, "Count, I'm a professional marriage broker, and I have a very nice young lady for you to marry. She is about twenty-one, pretty as a picture, very wealthy, from a good family, and a guaranteed virgin."

And the count says, "You know very well, my good man, that I need money, so a rich marriage is very welcome. The good family is also important. I could not come home to my family with anybody who was not from a good family. That she is pretty helps. The age is fine. But I won't take her because she is a virgin."

And the marriage broker says, "But Count! This is the rarest item you can find today."

And the count says, "That's exactly it. One whom no one has wanted before me, I don't want either."

And this is the story of the record companies when one comes to them with a work which nobody else has recorded. They don't want it either. They don't want virgins. They want the same works which have been recorded before, because I have tried without the slightest success to interest record companies in some very stunning and epoch-making works and haven't had any bite at all.

BADAL: Such as?

LEINSDORF: Such as the *Faust* of Schumann! Such as the complete *Le bour-*

geois gentilhomme of Strauss with narration! There are a variety of things which could really be great record productions, and nobody is interested.

BADAL: When Bruno Walter was eighty, he gave an interview in which he stressed the historical importance of recordings. Is this aspect of recording important to you?

LEINSDORF: Yes, of course! I think it is an important thing that performances can be recorded, and I think they will be as important as historical records are in old baptisteries where people go to find birth certificates. I read a fascinating story last Sunday about Sigmund Freud and his father's remarriage. These records were only to be found in Germany where his father lived, you know, in the synagogue in the archives. So records of the past are very interesting. If they are as accurate as we want them to be, I doubt very much. For instance, we have today facsimiles of the great composers' works. More are being issued, and I buy them up whenever they appear. But what the editors of the printed versions have done with these facsimiles! They have printed every slip of the pen which the composer made writing the music down. You know, even the greatest composer can make a writing error. And they did.

BADAL: Or make a blot on the paper.

LEINSDORF: Yes, and the quill may drain, you know; and sometimes I know that Beethoven's quill made a little spot and that people took this for either a note or some metronome marking. And I've seen these cases, so I'm a little bit skeptical. I think our imagination and our knowledge are a better guide and will lead us better into the past than too many records.

BADAL: Well, to me, the fact that I can hear Arthur Nikisch's Beethoven Fifth made in 1913, as awful as it sounds, the fact that I can hear him conduct anything at all—

LEINSDORF: Yes, but do you really know how he did it then?

BADAL: No, not really. I've nothing but an indication of tempo at best.

LEINSDORF: Yes, but this is only half the battle. Today if somebody imitated the tempi in a different context, they may be all wrong. Or the pitch may be all wrong. I'm not quibbling. I would love to have a record of Nikisch because I've not the foggiest notion of what he did. You are perfectly right. It is a fascinating—the ear equivalent of a glimpse, you know. I understand your fascination. You see, I have every good thing to say about recordings for the public. And of course, I think if people live away from the music centers—for instance, how many people live in cities where they can hear the great operas? So one day the video tapes will be in the same position as recording. People will buy the video tapes of operas, and they will get an idea of what the staging looked like. If they live in Idaho or the wilds of Arkansas, they will be able to get the great opera performances.

BADAL: You know, an actor who has been trained on the stage will tell you that when you start acting for the movies, it involves more than making a few practical adjustments. You really have to sit down and come to some aesthetic understanding of how one medium is different from the other. Is it the same for a conductor going from the concert hall to the recording studio?

LEINSDORF: Totally, totally, totally! It is the same thing. You see, your entire projection is different. Let us say that at the utmost extreme, you go into a very large hall which we encounter sometimes in touring—we get halls which sit six-, seven-, eight-thousand people—of course, your projection is one way. But when you project into a microphone which is a few feet away, your projection is entirely different. It is an intimate medium; and that, of course, allows for things which are different—compels you to be different in your approach.

BADAL: Music is an art that exists in time, and were you to conduct the same piece twice in a row, the second performance would be different from the first.

LEINSDORF: Definitely!

BADAL: But the recording is always going to be the same. I know there are some musicians who are disturbed by that.

LEINSDORF: There's no sense being disturbed. It is why I don't think that a recording can ever be anything more than a single performance. The recording is a performance, one performance of a work. And this is one of the reasons, this fact that a recording is only one performance which doesn't change, that I warn all young musicians not to study with recordings. You have served the perfect example.

BADAL: You and the members of your generation are really the first to embrace recordings. You take the generation of conductors before that, and they hated the process, and they hated the results.

LEINSDORF: Well, first of all, it was unbelievably difficult to do the four-minute, twenty-second bit when we worked with 78s. I made the first microgroove for RCA, the first long-play record in 1948, and I know the relief which we all felt. And then of course, when taping came in, you could splice. I made a few years ago a direct-to-disc recording which again brought back all the nervous tension of the old days.[2] I liked it very much for another reason. I liked the direct-to-disc because nobody can change your balances, you see. What you hear at the playback, that is the balance which nobody is going to change. I had enormous trouble with the people who went back from Boston to RCA and then doctored balances, particularly when RCA came out with this disastrous—what did they call it—Dynagroove, which was an unmitigated disaster. They ruined some of our records. Once in a while now when I get to Europe, people tell me that they get new pressings of some of these recordings which some other companies have made, and they're totally different records because they don't have this squashed-together dynamic range.

BADAL: How do you feel about digital?

LEINSDORF: I like it, I like it. I think they are constantly making technological improvements; and certainly we have nothing but improvements ahead of us, I'm quite sure. For instance, I got a pair of speakers recently from a friend of mine, who is behind the manufacture of these speakers, which are really tremendous. And all this I think is wonderful. When people have their own sound equipment! Also, the standard of the listener is going to be very much improved, because he will know what a first-class performance is, especially people who live in places where they don't have a first-class orchestra or where they don't have an opera company. I think it should raise the standards of the public. As I said, for the public, I think it is all to the good.

BADAL: Anyone who listens to a lot of records very quickly learns that certain kinds of performances don't repeat well while others do. For example, a live taping of a Furtwängler concert: the first time you hear it, it is the most dynamic thing you've ever heard, but the qualities that make it so dynamic don't repeat very well.

LEINSDORF: Let us face it. The vagaries don't repeat very well. It is as simple as that. I grew up with Furtwängler and can vouch for the enormous, grand tension and excitement which his every appearance created. But we were fully aware, with all our boundless admiration, that this was not the only way to do Beethoven or Brahms. As a matter of fact, it was highly, what should we say . . . the word "unorthodox" would not bother me . . . but it was something which was entirely bound up with the moment. It would be like a type of oratorical style that maybe William Jennings Bryan had enormous success with, but today if a contemporary politician should use that kind of oratory, it would not sit very well. I think that the style of Furtwängler was born out of a—

BADAL: It came down from Wagner, didn't it?

LEINSDORF: Well, I suppose so. But of course, there are things which Furtwängler did, even objectively speaking, better than anyone else, and they were not the kinds of things he was famous for. For instance, I find that he is the only conductor of whom I know who did the *Marriage of Figaro* overture correctly. Yes, he's the only one who did not go to the Indianapolis racetrack with that piece. No, you open here a tremendous can of worms with this question. There are pieces of which you get tired of, too, and other pieces you don't get tired of. This is really—this goes through the whole of music. There are people who wear well and people who don't wear well. And sometimes some of the most fascinating people don't wear well. There are performances which don't wear well. And this is really what you are bringing forth with some of these recordings you have.

BADAL: While we are talking about Furtwängler: one of the musical examples you discuss in *The Composer's Advocate* is the final presto in the last movement of Beethoven's Ninth Symphony. I remember in the book you said when Walter and Furtwängler were alive, you didn't know the proper question to ask as to why they played it the way they did. And when you knew the question, they weren't around to ask. Now when I read that passage, I played my Furtwängler and Walter recordings. There are still people who play it that way.

LEINSDORF: Oh, of course, of course. I remember, a friend of mine who is a musician spoke to Karajan when they did the Ninth Symphony. He asked him, "Tell me, have you read what Leinsdorf wrote?" Karajan had very nice things to say about the book; but at the end of the Ninth, I'm sure he does it the same way.

BADAL: The way he has always done the end.

LEINSDORF: I suppose. I cannot vouch for that. This example appeared in a short German essay of fifty-nine pages. It's really the way I started writing about these subjects. You see, there is no doubt about it. Taking the *maestoso* slowly as I've heard it all my life since I was a boy is wrong. There are no two ways about it. This is wrong. I mean, we are not here in the realm of individual liberty. I'm all in favor of, in fact, I want people to study with the composer so they should develop their own ways of reading the composer—which will mean that everyone will read the composer somewhat differently. But when something is wrong, it's wrong. And this is wrong. As I've analyzed it, you have three different proofs in the score. So here we are in the realm of a custom which is just a total error.

BADAL: And yet these recordings exist, and both men are highly respected.

LEINSDORF: Of course!

BADAL: The recordings are classics.

LEINSDORF: Of course! Winston Churchill was certainly not only respected but beloved and revered. And rightly so. But in 1914 or whenever it was, I think he was first lord of the admiralty then, he advocated a disaster at Gallipoli which wiped out I don't know how many British troops. It was an absolute, total abortive effort. Well, he's still a great man.

BADAL: But in your book, you advocate going back to the score; and doesn't the existence, the mere existence of those Walter and Furtwängler records lend a certain credibility to that misreading?

LEINSDORF: Well, this is exactly why I wrote the book! To say, don't take a great man's vagaries for the truth because he was a great man. You see, if a conductor had never listened to the Furtwängler-Walter version of the end of the Ninth, I think any normal musician reading Beethoven should come to the same conclusion which the score presents, as I've said, in triple proof. And then of course, people assume that because someone is successful that he is always right. Now, this is our misevaluation of success. A successful person can be just as wrong, at times, as an unsuccessful person.

BADAL: Or as an unsuccessful person can be right.

LEINSDORF: Yes, yes. You see, the element of success in any field is not necessarily always a direct indication of their being right or wrong.

BADAL: Do you listen to records?

LEINSDORF: I do not. Well, for pleasure I listen to records, but certainly not in any reference to the work I'm doing.

BADAL: What would you listen to?

LEINSDORF: If somebody gives me a Lieder recital of Richard Tauber, I would listen with the greatest of joy because it would be a great treat for me. Or a recording of Pablo Casals playing the cello! I would adore listening to that because it would be an enjoyment, a benefit, and so on and so forth.

BADAL: Media theorists say that people tend to accept the level of technology they are born into but regard all successive developments as dangerous. Do you see danger in the increased application of technology to music, or do you see a benefit?

LEINSDORF: The entire question goes right back to our seeming difficulties in making the best of the various industrial revolutions through which we live. Human beings have an infinite capacity of abusing what could be an unmitigated benefit. It is the same with all our technological advances. They can be of benefit and are much benefit; they can be abused, and they are much abused. Look at the airplane! How great it is to be able to go to California in five hours instead of three nights and two days as I had to do when I came to this country. But people abuse it. People abuse the airplane by overtiring themselves by flying too much—in my profession, certainly, and other professions as well. We human beings have the capacity of using technology for the best for our human race, and we have the capacity of abusing it. And we do both.

Notes

1. *Cadenza: A Musical Career* (Boston: Houghton Mifflin, 1976), and *The Composer's Advocate: A Radical Orthodoxy for Musicians* (New Haven, Conn.: Yale University Press, 1981).

2. Actually there were two discs recorded for Sheffield Lab: a Wagner collection and excerpts from Prokofiev's *Romeo and Juliet.*

CHRISTOPH VON DOHNÁNYI

⌐

BEFORE CHRISTOPH VON DOHNÁNYI succeeded Lorin Maazel at the Cleveland Orchestra helm in 1982, he possessed very little recording experience. His daunting reputation as an exponent of contemporary music was reflected in his limited discography by the two Berg operas on London and Henze's *Der Junge Lord,* an opera he had premiered in 1965, on Deutsche Grammophon. Except for a cycle of Mendelssohn symphonies—part analog, part digital—on London, there was little else. Something about the Dohnányi–Cleveland Orchestra combination aroused the interest of the major companies, however, and before the conductor became an exclusive London artist, the new partnership also appeared on Telarc and Teldec, making the ensemble the country's most recorded orchestra.

Dohnányi arrived in Cleveland for a round of meetings and ceremonial appearances in October 1983. Since the tightly packed series of media events fell behind schedule almost immediately, our interview took place while the Severance Hall public relations staff literally held reporters from a local television station at bay.

Dohnányi's 1983 projections as to the symphonic literature he would like to record proved entirely accurate; his opera plans, however, ran into some snags. His stated desire to record a Mozart opera with the Cleveland Orchestra has not yet been realized. Some rather complex plans to perform (at Blossom), record, and film Strauss's *Salome* and *Elektra* fell apart owing to soft funding for the films. In 1992, however, as part of the orchestra's seventy-fifth anniversary, London began a project to record Wagner's complete *Ring* cycle under Dohnányi's direction, the sessions for each opera following concert performances, over several years.

In 1990, London made a substantial financial investment in its future with the orchestra by building a removable platform in front of the Severance stage, extending over the seats on the auditorium floor, thus making the hall a far more satisfactory recording venue that it had been in the past.

"The sound is very good, very natural," remarked Dohnányi to me at the time. "When we know this place better after, maybe let's say, about six sessions or something like that, we will have an absolutely optimal recording situation there, I'm quite sure. And I think it's going to be one of the best places to record." ℘

Christoph von Dohnańyi conducts the Cleveland Orchestra. Photo by Peter Hastings.

BADAL: Maestro, the public tends to think of musicians in terms of what they record. Though I should know better, I'm just as bad as anyone else. When your appointment here was announced, people would come to me and say, "Well, who is he?" And I'd say, "Oh, he conducted that recording of Henze's *Der Junge Lord* on Deutsche Grammophon." Now, is this something that musicians today simply have to live with?

DOHNÁNYI: You have to live with it, I think. But, you know, it's just a question of whether it bothers you very much. There are some very good conductors who don't record at all. For instance, Celibidache doesn't do any recording, and he is one of the greatest. I think recording is very important for—it's more a matter of history, of . . . how do you call it . . . archive value. Because there are some people whom nobody knows these days who are very important. For instance, Leibowitz. You know the conductor René Leibowitz? There are some recordings, unfortunately not available in this country; but I think you can get them somehow— Beethoven, and so on—which are very important. And since nobody can hear Leibowitz anymore, these recordings I appreciate very much. Old Furtwängler! Some of the Toscaninis! And, for instance, there was a German conductor named Rosbaud, Hans Rosbaud, who really was a very fabulous conductor. He recorded very little.

BADAL: There are some.

DOHNÁNYI: There are some, but very few. He was a really great musician. And so I would say it is just a matter of some people recording a lot and not even caring very much about what they put down. Maybe the records sold well, but if you listen carefully, they don't sound too good. They don't mean much. Some record little, which doesn't mean they have to be better; but it's very hard to record a lot and be good. That's very hard because, you know, there is not so much money for recording, and things have to be pushed at sessions. Even if you play things before in concert, even if you rehearse them, it is very seldom that you are really happy after a recording. You know, we did some recordings—my operas and so on—and afterwards I said, "Oh, couldn't we do just two or three more hours? There's so much left to do." And you find some recordings by some of the most famous conductors of our day where bars are missing. Bars are missing! So one has to be very careful.

BADAL: What value do you think recordings have other than their archive importance?

DOHNÁNYI: You know, we do a Beethoven symphony, and somebody says,

"I want to take it home." That's like the tourist who says, "Let's have a picture." Went to Paris and took pictures; went to Lyons and took pictures, and so on. In a way this is what is happening with recordings. That's why, for me, recording is mainly a medium of report. It records something which is actual, something which is going on. So that's why I like live recordings, even if people are coughing. A recording is—how could I put it—a recording might be like a photograph rather than the real thing. It's very good for a conductor, for any musician, to record because it's a tremendous way of controlling your musicianship, your tempi and balances and things like that. But now some people, like Telarc for instance, record with very few microphones, and this makes a lot of difference because this is much more realistic.

BADAL: Is it possible for a conductor to make recordings too early?

DOHNÁNYI: I never pushed the idea of recording very much for myself. And I'm happy that I haven't recorded the Brahms symphonies yet and so on, because it is a matter of maturity, and I don't think it's too wise to put down Brahms and Beethoven and Mozart when you are twenty-eight.

BADAL: Do recordings have any educational value for the music-loving public?

DOHNÁNYI: Actually, the knowledge about music has been developed tremendously by recordings. There are so many people who know a lot about music who don't even play an instrument. On the other hand, I think a recording never really represents the realistic sound of the composition the way you hear it in concert. But I think we are coming to a certain point where recordings will achieve the proper balance with live concerts. You know, there was a time when recording just overwhelmed music, and everybody had to have everything: five *Tosca*s, five Beethoven Ninths, and so on. Now I think everything is a little more selective. If you consider, for instance, how radio developed, it was just a mess and trash, and you couldn't get any good music on it. And now it's something very different. And I think recording will become a much more artistic thing—if it can be paid for, you know, because it's tremendously expensive.

BADAL: Maestro, you're young enough to have grown up with recordings available to you. Did recorded music play any part in your early musical education?

DOHNÁNYI: No! Not at all.

BADAL: Are there any particular recordings you remember from when you were a boy that made an impression on you?

DOHNÁNYI: Very, very few. My parents didn't have many recordings, but we had some. You know, those 78s! I remember when I was a child, there were some recordings of Schlusnus singing. And, if course, we had some of the Beethovens, you know, things like that. But living in Berlin in those days, I went to concerts as many times as possible.

BADAL: Musically, that was an incredible time in Berlin.

DOHNÁNYI: Yes! So we didn't need recordings. We had a lot of chamber music at home, and we went to concerts.

BADAL: There's that very famous photograph taken in 1929 in Berlin of Walter, Klemperer, Kleiber, Toscanini, and Furtwängler standing in a row.

DOHNÁNYI: All those people, yes. But even in the time when I was brought up in the thirties, Furtwängler was there, and I went to his rehearsals and concerts. So I didn't listen much to recordings, actually.

BADAL: You haven't made too many recordings up to this point. Does the desire become stronger when you have an orchestra you can call your own?

DOHNÁNYI: Yes. You know, I did some recordings with the Vienna Philharmonic. This is a marvelous orchestra which I love very much. I did the Mendelssohn recordings because I wanted to study Mendelssohn. We didn't have much experience with Mendelssohn in Germany. When I was young, his music wasn't played, unfortunately, so I had to make up for that somehow. I studied Mendelssohn very carefully, and then I recorded those symphonies. And I also recorded some operas. But with the Cleveland Orchestra, it's different, of course. This is an orchestra which is so quick and so routined in recording. And I'm not now a young beginner anymore, so I'm looking forward to doing some important recording work.

BADAL: Are there any works which you have wanted to record and now feel that you can?

DOHNÁNYI: I am looking forward to doing a lot of the Beethovens, Dvořák; later maybe Brahms, Mozart, and Haydn. I mean, these are all very special. And if possible—I mean, it's just a matter of money—I would love to do some opera with the Cleveland Orchestra; I would love to do some Mozart operas.

BADAL: Lorin Maazel did one, the *Porgy and Bess*.

DOHNÁNYI: Yes, and I would love to do some Strauss maybe, and things like that.

BADAL: All of us in town are very excited about the Telarc recordings that you are going to make. It seems to me that I read once that one of the things you disliked about Hamburg was that you had to leave the city to make records.

DOHNÁNYI: Yes. I think to be able to record is very important for an orchestra because the musical level, the artistic level, the professional level must be very high. So I think it's a very healthy thing to be able to record. In Germany, actually, there are two orchestras which record. There's just the Berlin Philharmonic and the Bayerische Rundfunk. Some of the orchestras, you know, are rather well paid, and they just say, "OK, so other people record. We will just play," so the standard is not very high, technically speaking. In Hamburg, there were some marvelous musicians, but there were some other ones who really—you couldn't use them for recordings. And this situation you don't find over here in America.

BADAL: Music is an art which exists in time. If you conducted the same piece twice in a row, the second performance would be different from the first. But a recording is always going to be the same, and I know there are some musicians who are bothered by that. Does that bother you?

DOHNÁNYI: It does bother me, yes. It does bother me. That's why I didn't even have a record player, a machine, in my house. The people from Decca would come to my house and say, "How did you like the record?" And I would say, "You know, I have to be honest; I haven't heard it yet." My own recordings! And then they put a machine in my house, and I listened to them. Sometimes I liked them very much. For instance, two of the Mendelssohn symphonies, maybe three, I still like very much. But the other ones, I would like to do differently now, you know.

BADAL: Dare I ask which ones?

DOHNÁNYI: Yes, the "Lobgesang" for instance. The "Lobgesang," I think, even in the casting, it is not so perfect. I wasn't so close—I'm still not very close to this piece.

BADAL: It's a very difficult piece.

DOHNÁNYI: Very difficult piece. But the "Lobgesang" and the "Reformation" Symphony, those two are very difficult, and most likely I would have needed a little more time for them. But the "Italian" and "Scottish" I like very much. I also like the recording of the First, which is a beautiful piece.

BADAL: Anyone who listens to a lot of recordings learns something very quickly. Certain kinds of performances repeat over and over again very well. There are other kinds that don't. My favorite examples are always live radio tapes with Furtwängler. The first time you hear one, it is just the most incredibly dynamic and exciting thing you can imagine, but it doesn't repeat well.

DOHNÁNYI: You are perfectly right. The great recording conductors are not the ones who are the most individual conductors. Of course, that's why it is so hard for some people who try to imitate Furtwängler. It's very hard to do, and one shouldn't even try, because if he did something, in some way, it was very convincing. What I think is, if you are very individual, if you are a tremendous personality and you express something, at that moment people are very taken, you know, really just hypnotized. For instance, I know Furtwängler's Beethoven recordings, and I heard all the Beethovens, of course, many times in live concerts with him. It's a strange thing. Live he was much more convincing than on recordings, much more convincing. I don't agree with his picturing of the structure in Beethoven symphonies; I don't agree at all. Now, I think the Szell recordings are much closer, much closer to the picture of Beethoven than some of the Furtwänglers.

But you are perfectly right. If you listen to him later with a little more distance, then you say, "Why does he slow down so much here? What does it mean? Or why does he stop? Why doesn't he at least think about Beethoven's metronome markings?" You don't have to take the metronome markings in an absolute sense, but one thing should be considered very carefully. If Beethoven writes that something should be felt in one, you can't feel it in two. You can do one slower or one faster, but you can't feel two. And in this sense, metronomes are very important, I think, especially with Beethoven. There has been a lot of thinking about this, for instance, from the Kolisch Quartet. Leibowitz was one who was very close to this problem, and Szell very much so. And suddenly, you listen to Furtwängler; you listen, for instance, to Furtwängler's Beethoven Ninth Symphony.

BADAL: The Bayreuth one.

DOHNÁNYI: Yes. You know, you have the feeling the slow movement is falling apart in some way. It's just falling apart. But Beethoven has very,

very little metronome difference between the two tempi in the slow movement, and one should realize this. You can't do one very quickly and the other very slowly, you know. So in this sense, the metronome means a lot to me in Beethoven symphonies, even if you cannot play the music at the right speed because sometimes you just can't accomplish it technically.

BADAL: What kind of effect do you think recordings have on young conductors?

DOHNÁNYI: You know, I think if you are very young, it's good to be influenced by somebody. And that's one of our most difficult situations today, that young conductors look upon too many different so-called schools or *Schulen.* There was Gustav Mahler and Bruno Walter, and Bruno Walter didn't care about anybody else but Gustav Mahler. He was his master, you know. And there was Jochum to Furtwängler, and so on; and if you are young, that's very important. Some of the young conductors today, I have the feeling, can't bring any meaning to music anymore because they are listening to all those hundreds of records. I know a very famous conductor today, one of the most famous, who really puts together tapes of different kinds of interpretations, and then that's his master tape for studying a piece.

BADAL: Who were your idols when you were growing up?

DOHNÁNYI: You know, for me it was Furtwängler. I lived in Berlin, and it was Furtwängler. Then after the war, I coached in Frankfurt with Solti, who was very important to me, very important. Then when I was over here, I was very interested in what Lenny Bernstein did with music, because this was so different from anything you could experience in Europe. So it was rather fascinating up in Tanglewood.

BADAL: That was in the early fifties, right?

DOHNÁNYI: Yes. And Rosbaud was very important to me. He was in Munich, you know, when I studied. And then, I always—it's very interesting because Szell's work here was always very important to me. Even way before I was in touch with the Cleveland Orchestra, I was always following what he did, listening to concerts when he came, and so on, because, you know, he was—he tried to be so close to what was written. He was just very important to me.

BADAL: If you talk with an actor who has been trained on the stage but is now working in film, he'll tell you that there is more involved than simply doing things differently because the mediums are different. He'll say you really have to come to a philosophical understanding of how the theater is different from a movie. Does a conductor have to do the same thing when he moves from the concert hall into the recording studio?

DOHNÁNYI: No, no! I don't think so, because the difference is the actor has very seldom to face the same "libretto" in film as he does in the theater. If you write for film, that's one thing; if you write for the stage, it's different. Now if we would write music for recording—

BADAL: Which no one has ever done.

DOHNÁNYI: Which no one has ever done, you know.

BADAL: Except the rock groups, maybe.

DOHNÁNYI: Yes! If we would write music for electronic equipment, it would be very different, of course. I think that's the trouble, for instance, with opera on television. One should write an opera for television.

BADAL: There are a few who did.

DOHNÁNYI: Yes, there are some. Some people tried, but there is almost nothing. They just try to do *Butterfly* on television. This is very hard to do.

BADAL: Media theorists say that people tend to accept the level of technology that they are born into but regard all subsequent development as a threat. What dangers or benefits do you see with the increased application of technology to music?

DOHNÁNYI: There is a benefit. Of course, technology has helped increase the knowledge about music. But there is a tremendous danger, too. I think recordings put people in a position where they just lean back and listen. But that's something very different from a concert; it is more passive. It is like a voyeur. Our whole time is a voyeur time. You go to Africa, see those hungry people suffer, see those children with the flies in their eyes, you know. You take pictures and bring them home and say, "Isn't that terrible?" But that's as far as it goes. Our time is a voyeur time. And we are also voyeurs in music, and as a voyeur, you are not very creative. I think the media put too many people in this situation of not being creative. People who are just sitting back and listening to recordings would be better off and closer to music if they would go to the violin and the piano, have a friend over and do some chamber music, you know.

BADAL: I remember what a thrill it was for me the first time I could pick up the score to *The Marriage of Figaro* and really read it.

DOHNÁNYI: Things like that, things like that. But to be able to have a score, go for a walk, and read a string quartet! Very few people will do this because of all this Walkman business. They have their tapes. And I think this tremendous development of technological equipment cuts down creation, the ability of people to create themselves. But to stay with the philosophical point of view: the more information you receive, the greater your personality has to be; otherwise, you can't cope with it. You somehow get into this kind of situation where you suffer from feedback, you know, and you can't think anymore. Sometimes it's better not to go too far in being fed by other people's thought because then you don't think anymore. That's why some people don't compose anymore. It's a different situation. It's not only good, but it's not only bad.

SIMON RATTLE

ᴔ

Iᴛ ʜᴀs ʙᴇᴇɴ said that Simon Rattle is an old-fashioned conductor. In an age when many of his colleagues use orchestra appointments as mere rungs on the career ladder, he has remained contentedly with the City of Birmingham Orchestra since 1980, patiently developing both its potential and his own considerable talent. Reportedly, he also ignores lucrative offers to appear on other podiums, largely turning his back on the rat race of the guest conducting circuit.

Shrewdly aware of the problems he and other conductors of his generation face when they begin to record, he wisely selected Deryck Cooke's performing version of Mahler's Symphony No. 10, a work few have tackled on disc, for his first major project on EMI in 1980, a company for which he now records exclusively. Since then, he has consistently added interesting repertoire to his growing discography, such as works by Henze, Adams, and Weil. Though he has moved closer to the center of the so-called standard repertoire in recent years, he continues to shun Beethoven and Brahms in favor of Debussy, Janáček, Shostakovich, Sibelius, and Stravinsky. His decision to record his Glyndebourne Festival production of *Porgy and Bess* can be seen as both a confirmation of the opera's international status and a bold challenge to American domination in the Gershwin repertoire.

Rattle also demonstrates his individuality in his personal approach to working in the studio. Like Otto Klemperer before him, he has rebelled against the technology that makes it possible to assemble "perfect" performances from different takes of varying length and instead records large, multimovement works in single extended takes.

Whatever his attitude may be toward the practice now, Simon Rattle was obviously still guest conducting when he appeared with the Cleveland Orchestra in November of 1984. The rigors of his schedule dictated an interview in the lounge area of his downtown hotel. He maintained his good humor throughout, though clearly annoyed by the Muzak pouring from the ceiling speakers. ✌

Simon Rattle. Photo by Victoria Mihich. Courtesy of EMI.

BADAL: All the other conductors I've interviewed so far have been over fifty. If they grew up with recordings available to them at all, we're dealing with 78s. You, however, are young enough to have grown up with recordings available to you that represent the advanced states of the art, and I would think that would make a difference in your attitude toward them.

RATTLE: I'm sure that's true. But that being said, I think that 78s often give a more accurate picture of what an orchestra sounds like than many of the recordings I hear that are brought out now. I like that very clear, clean, honest sound of the 78s, which I also grew up with. My father had a very large collection of early records. Lots of Stokowski and Philadelphia. Those 78s sounded wonderful, actually, wonderful.

BADAL: Did recordings play any significant part in your musical education?

RATTLE: Oh, I think so. There was a great deal of music in Liverpool, and the orchestra played an enormously wide and adventurous selection of music. Between Liverpool and London there were always plenty of opportunities. But records obviously enabled me to explore even further. I started as a small child with an enormous love of twentieth-century music and worked backwards. And of course, in my teens I discovered that there were probably performances available on records that were more extraordinary than performances I would have a chance to hear, purely because the conductors were all dead. I did see Monteux as a small boy, and Barbirolli. So at least I had some contact there. But I never managed to see Klemperer, for instance—very, very sadly. But as a teenager, I found records of Furtwängler, Kleiber, Toscanini, Bruno Walter, of course, an enormous inspiration. Also, one felt that those records were produced honestly. I think that one can hear they are performances.

BADAL: Honestly from a technical standpoint?

RATTLE: And honestly from the point of view of giving you a performance as opposed to something snipped around. I find I listen to almost no modern recordings, although I do have them. What listening I do will tend to be to—I have lots of mono records.

BADAL: Were there any particular performances that made an impression on you?

RATTLE: I think I'm going to surprise you enormously. And I still think it's one of the great performances of the piece I've ever heard. It's the Brahms First Symphony with Stokowski, made very, very early on. Wonderful!

BADAL: With Stokowski?

RATTLE: Yes! You've never heard it?

BADAL: I don't think so.

RATTLE: Later in life there are very strange performances; but this one is marvelously propulsive, classical, straight, yet flexible. Marvelous!

BADAL: I guess Furtwängler was more straightforward when he was young, too. It was later that his performances became even more flexible.

RATTLE: That's interesting! I mean, everything he did was supported by such an extraordinary intellect. I think that people's—how shall I put it—people's conception of performances became straighter, and therefore Furtwängler will appear as more wayward.

BADAL: As a musician, how do you use recordings?

RATTLE: Sometimes I listen to recordings out of interest to find out how Mr. or Ms. X gets around a particular problem. That can be, sometimes, very interesting. I find them very useful when I don't know a piece at all, and I find them very useful when I know the piece extremely well—one that I have conducted a number of times. In between those extremes, I think they can be dangerous.

BADAL: You touch on something I'd like to get to in a minute.

RATTLE: Sadly, I can't do my answers in the same order as the questions.

BADAL: That's all right. In what way do you feel that recordings are dangerous?

RATTLE: I think the very availability of recordings has led to a rather embarrassing standardization of performances, and the range of what is considered the acceptable interpretation in many pieces has been very narrowed. I think people tend towards the mean, and I think recordings are culprits there. Hearing performances of many of the great masterpieces recorded now, one notices a great deal less individuality. It may be just that the conductors are less individual and less interesting. I think it's chicken and egg. One doesn't know which has come first. But I think recordings have been a blessing, and I think they have been a curse at the same time.

BADAL: As I said, everyone else I've interviewed has been over fifty, and they all speak very eloquently about the dangers of recordings for young conductors.

RATTLE: But never for themselves! Isn't that interesting!

BADAL: Well, I wouldn't quite say that. For example, Masur feels that young conductors may be inclined to imitate what they hear on recordings, and Leinsdorf feels they may be tempted to do the opposite of what they hear. Dohnányi says there is a time in your life when you have to imitate someone, that it's important when you're young to have someone to look up to. And he mentioned Bruno Walter to Mahler and Jochum to Furtwängler.

RATTLE: But then he's a very smart man indeed.

BADAL: But he said that today with so many recordings available to them, young conductors may have difficulty finding their own voices.

RATTLE: I think the difficulty is that, as a young conductor, it's possible to pick up idiosyncrasies without the discipline behind them. What one has to realize about Furtwängler's interpretations is that they were based on an extraordinary bedrock of intellect, and there was nothing that man didn't know about the structure of the music, about the intellectual hard core. He wasn't an instinctive musician like Toscanini or Stokowski, for instance. He understood all the foundations of harmony, counterpoint, and structure, and so his departures were all structural and all organic to the music. As a young conductor, you can listen, and it's like being set free. But, of course, to imitate it is very dangerous because one has to start once again from the—one has to go from the bottom up. Just as Schoenberg was, of course, the most rigorous conventional-harmony teacher of the century! His pupils were not allowed to go beyond it until he felt they were absolutely secure and had that background to fall back on. Atonality without that is just an indulgence.

BADAL: Somehow one feels that Mengelberg's departures were not as structurally motivated as Furtwängler's.

RATTLE: But we rarely hear Mengelberg conducting except as a very old man. Having only heard Klemperer, seeing him conduct on television, as a very old and sick man, it was a revelation to hear recordings from the twenties.

BADAL: Or some of the live performances from his Hungarian days.

RATTLE: Or even the earlier things with the Vienna Symphony Orchestra. One sees an entirely different person. I mean, one understands why Klemperer and Boulez became so close. Many, many similarities! And so, in these ways, recordings can also give a distorted picture. There is no doubt that a record is a recording of an event in a moment of time, reflecting only the choices available to one at that time. When I come to recording certain pieces I've already recorded, it will be very interesting to see. Even now when I listen back to things I recorded three or four years ago! I don't find them unacceptable, but I do sometimes think, "Oh, foolish young man." Just purely because things change. As a conductor, one has to be going—one has to be changing all the time. I think the greatest danger of recording is that one can be standardized and that one can think having done a piece, that then, there it is! And of course, music is always changing; it was not meant to be captured; it was not meant to be the same each time. Music was not meant to sound like gramophone records.

BADAL: I gather from what you've said that the historical aspect of recording is very important to you.

RATTLE: I think it is important to listen to old recordings and not say when those things come unexpectedly upon you, "Oh, but that's ridiculous." Actually sit and ponder why, at that particular time, that was deemed to be necessary.

BADAL: Have you ever heard the recordings of Nikisch?

RATTLE: Oh, yes!

BADAL: Extraordinary!

RATTLE: But if one hears Oskar Fried's recordings of Mahler—despite the fact that one can hear the double basses are played by four tubas—there is still a flexibility which is of a tradition almost lost. In fact, I've the feeling that Toscanini, who was without doubt one of the most important musicians of the century, that his recordings came upon an unsuspecting world and created a kind of mania of rigidity.

BADAL: But most of his recordings come from his later years. There is a record of his first recordings made in 1921 with the La Scala Orchestra.

RATTLE: I'm sure that they will be very different, just as Stravinsky's early recordings are very different. I mean, Stravinsky's recordings of his own works seem to have persuaded an entire generation to play his music like gravel and at twice the speed. Indeed, I've seen occasions where conductors have very faithfully listened to the records of Stravinsky and taken the wrong notes that the players have played in those recordings and changed the notes in the score. They've also taken some of the ludicrous tempos that either he or possibly Robert Craft took. There's an extraordinary recording of the *Symphony in Three Movements* made by the New York Philharmonic just after the work's premiere in 1945, and one hears what a marvelous conductor Stravinsky was. And of course, in those days the New York Philharmonic was a great orchestra. It's full of color, life, passion, and singing as well.

BADAL: How do you feel about working in the studio? Do you, for example, like the principle of the long take?

RATTLE: I will no longer record works that have not been played by the orchestra and myself many times in performance. And apart from absolute disasters, I will not cut in. The new cycle of Sibelius recordings which we've started—we did the Second during the summer, and we decided from that time onwards that we would do those recordings in takes of an entire symphony.

BADAL: Not just individual movements?

RATTLE: Not split into movements! The Second is just about to come out, and I think you can tell that we made—we had three sessions. Having rehearsed frantically first, we then made a take of the entire symphony, listened to it, worked through the evening, and then came back the next morning and made another take of the whole symphony. What the effect is for the musicians and myself is that we forget we are in a recording studio, which is one of the hardest things to do. It felt to us like a performance, as though we were performing for each other as a kind of ideal audience who understood what each other wanted. We were all very excited by the cumulative sense of the recording and the feeling that this is how we play, at that moment that was what we wanted, and that there was nothing cosmetic in the process.

BADAL: Did you record Britten's *War Requiem* that way?

RATTLE: There are some pieces one is simply not able to—

BADAL: You'd have a hell of a time recording an opera.

RATTLE: I know. Well, I mean, if you've heard Giulini's *Falstaff*, which is taken from live performances, it's wonderful! The *War Requiem* was split into a number of sections with chamber orchestra, a number of sections with large orchestra and chorus, and it was frantically difficult to record because of that. The contrast of the piece is implicit in the two ensembles. It is very difficult to spend three hours recording only the choral sections, very hard.

BADAL: I imagine you have to be very clear in your own mind where each section fits into the whole.

RATTLE: We had done it many times. And don't forget that the orchestra and the chorus did, among other things, the first performance of that piece. So there are still many of the orchestra who can remember seeing these scrawly pencil-written parts and scrambling their way through the Libera Me believing they'd never seen anything quite as difficult. And the orchestra had played the piece, extraordinarily, at least twice a season every year since the first performance because it's been an enormously played piece in England. We had played the piece five or six times over the course of two years.

BADAL: I think anyone who listens to records and attends concerts has had the experience of hearing a recorded performance and thinking, "I don't care for that," but if he had heard the same artist perform the piece live, he may have accepted it.

RATTLE: That is precisely, of course, one of the reasons for the lack of risk-taking in recordings, because every musician realizes that. . . . Any musician is probably going to hate his own recordings. That's one of those things. By the time they come out, it's always a year or so after you've made them, and one has always moved on. I can't pretend I listen to my records. There are some I have never even heard apart from actually approving the final pressings. I use recording, of course, for a different purpose—in orchestra building. I mean, orchestra building is very out of fashion these days. Conductors tend to want to make their careers as guest artists, running backwards and forwards, going two weeks here, two weeks there, to all the great and prestigious orchestras.

BADAL: That's one of the reasons we're so pleased with our new music director in Cleveland. Clearly, he doesn't think that way.

RATTLE: Thank goodness! There is very, very little pleasure in guest conducting. There's very little music making. You can do your best, but it's always a very suspicious situation. It's always a matter of just papering over cracks. When I went to Birmingham four years ago, I didn't actually dream at that time that this would be something that I would consider spending many, many years working with. The improvement and the passion of the musicians has proved to be such that—

BADAL: And you think recordings play a part in this?

RATTLE: I think so. It's a way of everybody hearing each other and hearing where they are. I found, particularly when we began working, that after each recording there was a dramatic jump in the awareness and the standard of the orchestra. I use recording now as a tool in orchestra building, as well as a remarkable discipline for us and as a place where one simply has to sort out the problems. It's an enormous incentive for everybody to be working their best. I think that's what one must be aiming for with an orchestra all the time. Give them opportunities and places where they must give their best and better. And then one can jump from plane to plane. As one reaches a certain height, then that is the expected standard. Then one can move on from there, and for me, in a way, that is the most important aspect of my recording.

BADAL: I've noticed that when young conductors begin to record, they tend to concentrate on the fringes of the repertoire. In your own case, Britten and Janáček.

RATTLE: You know, you may think that's the fringe of the repertoire, but—

BADAL: Would you do a Beethoven symphony?

RATTLE: What would be the point? There's no point in recording something unless it is good. No! I think there'd be no point. I think very often there are some pieces that are exceptionally difficult for conductors, among them Beethoven symphonies. I think a recording has got to be an event. I mean, there's no point—I love conducting Beethoven, but there's no point in recording an interpretation which is not, in some sense, finished. As a permanent record, I don't see the point.

BADAL: Are you speaking purely for your own satisfaction, or is there also the realization that every great conductor has recorded them?

RATTLE: I think it's simpler than that. I just think that you have a duty towards that music and that you have to be able to look that music straight in the face without being embarrassed. I wouldn't want to inflict another second- or third-rate recording of Beethoven's Seventh on anyone. I think there are plenty of second- or third-rate recordings without my adding another one. Who knows, it could be worse.

BADAL: If you talk to an actor who was trained on the stage, he will tell you that if you start making movies, you have to come to a philosophical understanding of how the mediums are different from each other. Is it the same for a conductor moving from the concert hall into the studio?

RATTLE: I used to think that, but now I try to make them as similar as possible. I think you can choose to take Muti's approach, which is to work on each bar until it's perfect and then go to the next bar, or you can choose to say, this is a performance and no amount of perfection and polish will make it a better performance. It may give it more perfection and polish. But a piece of music is an entity, and I think it does a disservice to the music to cut it into little, tiny bits and then pretend when it's stitched together that it's going to be anything more than a stitching. You couldn't do that to a human being.

BADAL: Media theorists say that people tend to accept the level of technology they are born into but regard further developments as dangerous. What dangers to music do you see from the application of technology?

RATTLE: I think this abortion which is playing over us at the moment is one of the great dangers—the fact that everyone hears music as wallpaper all the time. In supermarkets, hotels; you name it. I think there's an enormous danger that audiences will tend to go to concerts wanting to be soothed and hear nice, gentle wallpaper. Sometimes I think in some American cities the audiences sound to me as if they're going to a movie. They talk, they rustle, they cough. It is as though the concert is a background, an entertainment to be switched on and switched off.

BADAL: It's like the way the audiences at La Scala behaved in the nineteenth century.

RATTLE: But they were involved in the music. It's different. They were shouting and screaming about, but that's different.

BADAL: Do you see any benefits to music from technology?

RATTLE: If records raise the standard of orchestral playing, or if they raise the standard of what people expect. They can, however, act as a contraceptive to musicians who may become too terrified to take a risk or play a wrong note. So I think there are equal benefits and dangers. If records become something that dampens your sense of adventure about music making, then I think they're probably doing a criminal act. If they bring music to a wider audience, then they are giving untold benefits.

CHARLES DUTOIT

ॐ

CHARLES DUTOIT'S CAREER in the studio demonstrates a particularly interesting facet of the recording business: that in some cases, labels and the public want to link the nationality of the conductor with the nationality of the composer—Italians for Rossini, French for Ravel. A French-Swiss musician born in Lausanne, Dutoit grew up in a musical atmosphere dominated by Ernest Ansermet, and he acknowledges the late conductor of the Orchestre de la Suisse Romande as one of the principal influences in his own musical development.

As music director of the Montreal Symphony Orchestra, Dutoit's repertoire naturally embraces the entire field of symphonic literature. However, as an exclusive artist on London (the same label that had enjoyed Ansermet's services for thirty years), he found himself, partially of his own choosing, taking over the same French composers with whom his countryman had been so firmly identified. Though he rightly insisted in our March 1985 interview that he and his orchestra were moving into other areas on disc, a decade later much of his recorded repertoire continues to be the repertoire of Ansermet: the French masters, the Russian Romantics, and the early moderns, such as Bartók, Stravinsky, and Prokofiev.

Besides being responsible for the week's concerts in Severance Hall, Dutoit was taking the Cleveland Orchestra on a swing through the South, a circumstance that placed him in the unenviable position of preparing an enormous amount of material in very little time. The Severance public relations staff squeezed this interview between Dutoit's intensely busy morning rehearsal (judging from the towel draped over his shoulders) and his lunch. In spite of the less-than-ideal conditions, Dutoit responded to questions with genuine enthusiasm. Following the interview, the maestro was lunching with Krystian Zimerman, soloist for the week's concerts, and the pianist sat quietly at the other end of the office, hence Dutoit's occasional references to him. ॐ

Charles Dutoit. Photo by Jim Steere. Courtesy of the Orchestre Symphonique de Montréal.

BADAL: Maestro, many of the older conductors, men born in the last century, loathed making records, they hated the process, and they hated the results. You, however, are young enough to have grown up with recordings available to you that represented a fairly advanced state of the art. Does that make your attitude toward records different from the older generation's?

DUTOIT: Well, first of all I don't think it has to do only with the older generation of conductors. I know many of my colleagues and young soloists, such as for instance, Krystian Zimerman who is playing this week with me—he hates recordings. So I don't think it's a conflict of generations. It's mainly, I think, the approach that someone takes toward the technology. I personally love to make recordings, especially when I can do it on my own terms. I don't like to go and record as a guest conductor, for instance. I have done a lot of records in London, in Paris and Geneva, even in Los Angeles, where I was a guest conductor, and I prepared the orchestra in two days and had to make a record. And I should say that this is not very satisfactory. At least one should be able to—you know, whenever you make a recording, you do the best you can. As a guest conductor, you can't do the best you can because you have to compromise constantly with an orchestra—to adjust to their technique somehow. You cannot really change things in one or two days, you know.

BADAL: The orchestra has its own personality.

DUTOIT: Yes, but some orchestras, especially the London ones, you would expect to be flexible because they play such an enormous amount of music with so many different conductors, but in fact, it's just the contrary. You can't just make a London orchestra play differently. They have their own way to play, and that's it! So I don't record any longer in London. My latest and greatest pleasure has been to record in Montreal because there I could form the orchestra the way I wanted in order to record. There was a long preparation as far as the quality of sound was concerned, as far as the very subtle balance was concerned. Then I was asked to record for London everywhere, and I told them, "Well, you know, I think you should come to Montreal, because you will get a better result there than with any orchestra I can conduct as a guest." Not because—I don't want to say that the orchestra is better than the others, but I have more control of the quality.

BADAL: They know you better.

DUTOIT: Of course, and I can train them to go into the studio, and so. London came and they were very impressed and interested in pursuing something with us there. And this has, of course, all of this has an enormous importance today because of the technology—the new technology, digital and compact discs. There is no noise whatsoever, and now a middle-of-the-road orchestra recording on compact discs doesn't come off so well. Before there was more of a generalized sound, you know, something in the middle. Now you see, that sound is so—this technology gives us such a fantastic spectrum; all the colors come out, and so on. So we really have to care very much about the quality of the orchestra.

BADAL: Does this create a problem for the listener who is used to hearing the incredible clarity of a CD and doesn't hear the same thing in a concert hall?

DUTOIT: Oh well, this the eternal problem, you know: the difference between recordings and the concert hall. I think they are two different fields. First of all, we go to a concert hall, and that's it! It's a moment in our life. We live this concert, and nothing will ever replace that. The performance will be what it is. And there is a different kind of involvement at a concert, both for the public and for the orchestra. There is more communication among all of us. You play a concert, and you know that it's one moment. A recording is—can be also one moment. It is, in fact, one moment, especially here in America where we record so fast, so quickly that it's actually like a concert performance.

BADAL: It's a repeatable moment, though.

DUTOIT: That's what I mean. So the record listener, on the other hand, has a different perspective because he listens to a record, and then again and again and again. He gets used to it. So obviously from the listener's point of view, a record is not the same thing as a concert. I don't know any record fan who doesn't like to go to concerts because the people who really care about music—I'm not talking about fanatics, you know, people who are hi-fi fiends. I think that's more an attitude than anything else. They are so crazy about their equipment and this and that and so. But somebody who dearly likes music and buys a record because he loves a piece, or he loves an orchestra, or a soloist, or a conductor, will go with a lot of understanding to a concert. I have never heard anyone tell me, "Oh, it's not as good as on the record." Although I must say that when we were in Europe not long ago with the Montreal Symphony, I said to the orchestra, "Listen, my friends! You had better be very good, because you know, your reputation in Europe has been made through some wonderful records. Now, if you don't play as well as you record, obviously people will be disappointed." But actually they were just as good. Sometimes even better!

BADAL: Did recordings play a role in your musical education?

DUTOIT: Well, yes and no. Actually, you see, I came to music by listening to some records which impressed me very much. One of the very first ones was the Beethoven Violin Concerto with Kreisler. It was still on the 78s you know. . . . Because I was studying the violin, I listened to the record. I had never the pleasure to hear Kreisler personally, but that performance was really so unbelievable that I fell in love, you know, with the concerto and the violinist. He was my hero during my young days. And then not long afterwards, I heard the very first LPs; you know, London records. I remember the labels were orange. They were London records, Decca in Europe; and they were Boyd Neel, the Brandenburg Concerti. And one of the very first LPs that I received—because I won a little contest on the radio, you know, and we had to guess something—was Clemens Krauss conducting the Vienna Philharmonic in *Don Juan* and *Till Eulenspiegel.* And also on record. Some friends of mine had these Saturday evening sessions where we had a little glass of wine, or coffee, or lemonade or whatever, and we listened to records. And that is how I came across the music of Stravinsky like *Les Noces.* So obviously records played a role in my youth, although they were not as popular as they are now, you know.

BADAL: Today the public tends to think of any musical artist in terms of what he records. I suppose any musician has to be aware of the impact of recordings, especially when it comes to building a career. Is this something you just have to live with whether you like it or not?

DUTOIT: Well, I think there is a certain level of career today which has to do with the recording business. You know, the level of your career changes when you make recordings. I can see some artists, marvelous first-class musicians, who are not recording. They tend to have careers a little hidden, you know, whereas the ones who are recording are obviously more exposed. And this seems to be obvious and doesn't need any explanation, because these recordings are played all over the world on the radio, you know, and so obviously people get used to names. Actually, there are very few artists who have exclusive contracts with record companies. It is very amazing to see if you take the five largest or most important labels how many exclusive artists they have. It's very few. You know, today you look at Deutsche Grammophon, and they have, what, two or three conductors, one or two pianists, one violinist. My own company, London, has three conductors: Solti, Chailly, and myself.

BADAL: And Dohnányi.

DUTOIT: Yes, but he is not exclusive.[1] He has made some records with them, but he is not—at least I think he has made recordings for different labels. Record companies tend to—they want to sell their records. So therefore, they make more publicity, more promotion, and obviously it gives the artist better exposure and ultimately a better career.

BADAL: I can think of certain artists who were exposed too widely too early.

DUTOIT: Oh, yes, well this is something else. You see, if now you talk about the timing, I tend to agree with you. But that's changing because record companies went through some problems in recent years, and I think they are a little more selective now than they used to be. They used to produce so many records and take artists at, what you call it, cradle?

BADAL: Cradle robbers.

DUTOIT: Yes, you know? Whenever they heard about someone, they would have them make records. Somehow I think it's wrong to start too early. It's wrong to start too early, at least as a conductor anyway. I'm not talking about a violinist, you know. A violinist can play beautifully at sixteen or at forty-five because he plays his own instrument. But a conductor needs that much experience, and I don't think he can pretend to be a good conductor very early. And so therefore, a conductor should not record too soon.

BADAL: How do you use recordings as an artist? Do you listen to them?

DUTOIT: I don't really listen to records. I listen, however, to cassettes, especially when I'm flying. One of the reasons is that sometimes I have to know a singer or an opera, or a timing or something like that. So usually when I am flying I take a few cassettes with me, and I listen to those cassettes on the plane. Sometimes I receive a lot of cassettes, of course, because many soloists, but especially young people, send cassettes and things like that, and so I listen. Many operas! I like to get to know some singers. But you see, when I am at home and I have some free time, I don't listen to music because I like to do something else: to read, to be home with my wife, to go to a museum, to go to the theater. And I go to some concerts when I have friends over and I feel I can learn something from a great artist who is playing somewhere, you know. Otherwise I don't have really much time to listen, and I don't really use recordings professionally except when I have a specific problem to solve. You know, for instance, a phrasing or a problem I'm not sure—let me give you a specific example. There is in Janáček a piece called *Taras Bulba*.

BADAL: A wonderful piece.

DUTOIT: It's a wonderful piece! But in *Taras Bulba* there is a bar, a transition between two tempi in the first part which I can't understand. I don't understand what the composer wants to do. It doesn't work one way or the other. You know, mathematically there is something wrong there. And I just couldn't solve this problem. Now if I were living at the time of Bach or in the nineteenth century, I would have gone to—like Bach went to Lübeck to meet Buxtehude, you know, because there was no alternative. Today, we can buy records and have access to some solutions which great artists have resolved. And I think,why shouldn't we take advantage of that? And you know, listening to Kubelik or Karel Ančerl, who have been involved with this music all their lives, I found the solution. You see, that was a very specific thing, this rhythmic little thing. Because what Janáček thought is not clear. The writing is not clear. It is very clumsy, the way it is written. So this is one example.

BADAL: How important is the historical aspect of recordings to you?

DUTOIT: Oh, I think it's extraordinary, of course. Although I think it's very difficult to frankly and honestly say what we can learn, for instance, from a—no, not what we can learn, we can always learn, but what we could take and *imitate,* try to do again, from a Furtwängler interpretation. I don't believe we can. This is the problem with records; it's the danger that I feel. Recording stops the development. A recording belongs to a specific time and specific moment in an artist's life. And for instance, there are many things in a Furtwängler performance which we couldn't do now—some very slow tempi. We cannot imitate that because we don't have the same blood pressure; we don't have the same style of life; we don't have—it's a different world, you know, so if you don't live intensely in that world, then you cannot take anything from it and try to imitate it.

BADAL: Of course if it were not for recordings, we would not know how older conductors used portamento, how they did it and where they did it.

DUTOIT: That's right, that's right. But, on the other hand, one thing is amazing. I used to listen to a lot of great old pianists and violinists. Today, we talk about the great techniques of these young people, their musicality and so on. We say, "Oh well, they have fantastic technique." But the older people had better technique. These fantastic pianists, starting with Busoni and Rachmaninov and even before, you know. The equipment was unbelievable.

BADAL: There was a time when orchestras had very strong national characteristics. Those national characteristics don't seem to exist quite so much any more, except for a few obvious cases like the Vienna Philharmonic. Do you think recordings played any role in this?

DUTOIT: Yes and no. We are now in America, and in America every music director has to be—has to have a wide repertoire because he works so much with his own orchestra. And if you are German or if you are Italian, you could not do only your own music, you know. I mean, we have to do so much music, and obviously we train the orchestra to be also flexible in style. We play much more music than before, and obviously it's wonderful on the one hand and also maybe a pity on the other because the personality of the orchestra is wider but with less individuality. Now, as you said, in Vienna—

BADAL: Some of the East German orchestras also tend to sound as they used to.

DUTOIT: That's right! Dresden, Leipzig. Dresden especially. But the Vienna Philharmonic, we should remember, is an opera orchestra. They play very few concerts, they have no music director, they have no conductor. They give, I think, eight or ten subscription concerts a year. That's all! And they usually play late Romantic music. They hardly play modern pieces. They have also only Viennese people in the orchestra, and they are all pupils of this one and that one. So it's really a very, very Viennese affair. So obviously they are not very flexible. And their wind school is also very awkward to me and to many other of my colleagues. But when they play their own repertoire, I don't think anyone can come close to them, you know. But of course, they are limited in the range of the repertoire they do well, as I said. You know. I mean, I'm doing music from Monteverdi on. Nearly everything! I don't say I do everything *well* because obviously nobody can, but I'm very curious; I could not live with only ten symphonies and a few other pieces.

Careers before were different. When you think of Furtwängler or Bruno Walter, they are known today for a certain repertoire. That doesn't mean they didn't do anything else, because if you see what Furtwängler did in his younger days—he did some Ravel and things like that, you know. I don't know whether it was good or not, but obviously he was a real, traditional German conductor. Today we are a little more international, and maybe recordings also had something to do with that. I'm not quite sure, though, if it's the recording business which has changed things or just the fact that interest in music in general has developed all over the world. There is more demand for music. I was in Philadelphia last week;

and not that long ago, maybe thirty years ago, the orchestra had a very short season. They were playing a few weeks, you know, and they were trying to get jobs here and jobs there in order to survive. So the demand was not great. Today, all these orchestras have fifty-two-week contracts, and they have to play a lot of concerts and a lot of music. You see, I think it's the times. It's a time where everyone is more curious. There is a lot of information going around with the media, with radio and television and everything. We tend to be a little more international.

BADAL: You stress that today a conductor has to have a much wider repertoire. Yet people who know you only from recordings would think of you as a conductor of French and Russian repertoire. Is that by your choice?

DUTOIT: I must tell you that first of all, I was born in Lausanne, in Switzerland, and I was greatly influenced by Ernest Ansermet, who was the maestro there. Although I had never a lesson from him, I'd been following his work for many years, and he was my example, my mentor—not only as a musician, but also intellectually. You know, his mind, his way of looking at things and trying to understand things. He was one of the last humanists, and that approach very much influenced me. Now, when I arrived in Montreal, which is, as you know, a French city, I started to work with the orchestra in many fields. We did a lot of things. But then I was asked to record for London. Now, the question of repertoire was the number one question, as in every company. Now you see, it is not only because I have a French name, it is also because I came from that background of Ansermet who was an exclusive London record artist for thirty-five years. Ansermet, as you know, was connected with all this beginning-of-the-century music—not only French, but Stravinsky, Bartók, Hindemith, Falla. You know, all the living composers. He conducted the first performances of most of these pieces and actually recorded them for the first time himself. Now, when he died, there was a big gap in the catalogue—not only because of him, but because all the French conductors died. All these conductors died. There is nobody left. Think of that great school: Monteux, Munch, Clutyens, Inghelbrecht, Desormière, Ansermet, Wolff. I mean, so many! That was a fantastic school, and there is nobody left. In France today, you have no conductor of world class except Boulez. But Boulez is not really a conductor in that sense; you don't think of Boulez as a conductor like you think of Munch or Karajan. He is a personality, and he does so many things. So one reason why we started with French music was the gap of genuine feeling for that kind of repertoire. You know, today you hear some Ravel played by a London orchestra and an Australian conductor, and this can be a beautiful performance. But that very specific touch of color and sensitivity, the genuine thing is missing. I don't say that it's right or wrong, but it used to be like this, you know, when you had Clutyens and Munch doing this music. It was a time which has disappeared. So what we are trying to do, actually, is fill this gap. It is not a restriction, because things are changing already. We have recorded, as you say, some Russian repertoire, and we are going to record some English music and also some Mendelssohn.

BADAL: What English music are you going to record?

DUTOIT: Well, we are going to do some Elgar, and we will do *The Planets* next fall. We are changing our image, you know; but as I said, we decided to fill this gap. But there was also the marketing point of view. There is no reason to record today unless you do first-class recordings. Otherwise what is the point? There are so many records. I mean, we can play very well the Mahler First Symphony, which we have done on tour with great success. Now, if I record the Mahler symphony today, it will have no impact whatsoever because there are so many people who have recorded Mahler, and they certainly have a better image for it. Maybe one day we will. But when we started recording, that was the beginning of the crisis in the recording business, so I thought, well, we have to be very careful to do not just another record but something which will go to the top right away and bring us the kind of recognition which will encourage the record company to stay with us. You know, this is very important because to pay an orchestra today is enormously expensive. So this combination of a mercantile approach and artistic approach I think is very important for a music director. I'm sure Krystian doesn't have these problems because he, himself, is a pianist; but as a music director, I have responsibility toward the city where I work and the orchestra. If I want to put them on the map, I've got to play the game.

BADAL: Media theorists say that people tend to accept the level of technology they are born into but regard successive developments as a danger. Do you see any danger from the increased application of technology to music?

DUTOIT: Well, you see, it's not just today's problem. It has always been the problem of the relationship between a musician and this technology, and I think most musicians were very—we started this interview with this—were very suspicious of this technology. They hated to make records. But I personally don't see any danger. If there is any danger, it is up to us to just react to it the right way, you know. For instance—again I'm talking about Krystian because we're so different—he doesn't want to record. He hates the business, and he does very few concerts. He wants to do only what he wants, when he likes and so on. I myself am much more open to these technologies and these things. I don't really see danger as long as we master our own situation, and have to live with them, you know. The digital system is just a digital system, and that's it. What can you change?

I can answer this way. You know, thirty years ago when I was in Switzerland, people were scared to death because of the Americanism. You know, after the war we said "Oh, gee! We have our traditions, we don't like to think about money. We are not materialistic; we are educated in a certain way." And then we were so scared because the Americans came over to Europe, and they had so much money, you know, and they were talking about their wonderful houses and their wonderful refrigerators and their televisions and all these things. We thought that was so silly, and that was such a bad way to talk because there are other values. And we still think the same way; but we cannot avoid the fact that now everybody has a television, and everybody has a refrigerator, and everybody has a car. But still we have to accept this, and we have to also accept these new technologies. I think it's wonderful what we can do today with the recordings, digital and compact discs, and so on. I don't know if we are going to improve on this. I don't see how. It is so beautiful—you know, what we can do today. But I think it would be silly for me to say that I am against these developments, because the world is going ahead, and we have to live with that.

Note

1. At the time Christoph von Dohnányi was not an exclusive artist with London; now he is.

CHRISTOPHER HOGWOOD

౫

CHRISTOPHER HOGWOOD BELONGS to a relatively new, flourishing group of scholar-performers. Originally trained as a harpsichordist, he later branched out into conducting, radio work, and writing. As founder of the Academy of Ancient Music in 1973, he has played a leading role in what has been variously described as the "original instrument" or "authentic performance" movement.

Hogwood sees recording as both a vehicle for promoting, or at least presenting, the ongoing scholarship in the area of authentic performance and an opportunity for experimentation with performing practices. His extensive discography for L'Oiseau-Lyre includes such items as a wide ranging exploration of Vivaldi, the complete symphonies of Mozart, and a variety of compositions by Handel, his work with the latter augmented by his in-depth study *Handel,* published by Thames and Hudson in 1985 for the tercentenary of the composer's birth.

Book and author arrived in Cleveland at about the same time during the summer of 1985. Scheduled to lead some Handel programs in June at Blossom, Hogwood faced the interesting challenge of training a thoroughly modern ensemble in the niceties of proper eighteenth-century style. Through some extraordinary stroke of luck, his schedule proved far less hectic than is the norm during the summer season, and our interview ambled along at a leisurely pace with ample time to fully explore the issues raised. The Beethoven symphony cycle to which he refers—the first from a "specialist" —began appearing shortly after his Blossom concerts. ౫

BADAL: Almost every conductor I've talked to, no matter how many records he may have made, is ambivalent about the ultimate worth of the product. Rightly or wrongly, the public regards you as a specialist promoting

Christopher Hogwood conducts the Cleveland Orchestra at the Blossom Music Center. Photo by Peter Hastings.

a specific cause as far as the performance of a certain repertoire is concerned. It occurs to me, therefore, that you might view recordings as allies.

HOGWOOD: Yes. I'm certainly not ambivalent about them. I can't see why people should be, unless they have a particularly strong attachment to the value of audience response. But I think audiences, the musical public, are now very aware of what a record represents—a type of photograph of an event. And rather like a Victorian studio photograph, it can be either candid, or posed, or superimposed, or retouched. It can be anything you want from the most honest to the most—many people would say—dishonest. The ultimate value of some recordings is nil from the moment they're made, as, of course, are many family snapshots negated by the simple fact of who made them and when. On the other hand, there are many photographs which I think will live forever although they were only moments in time. It depends on the power of the photographer, the scenes, the subject, the surrounding circumstances, the rarity, the insight it gives. One can't say now how many records will or should survive. You can play games of going on to a desert island with ten records that you would care to live with, but these usually reflect more on you than the records. A recording is an artifact which is not a live performance and is only a measure of work in progress. I think for most people—certainly everything that is being done in exploratory areas like contemporary music, like a lot of jazz, like a great deal of the historic movement at the moment—it is merely a way of assessing work in process: the state of the art. For us, particularly working with early instruments, the recording situation is a laboratory, and what comes out of it is a laboratory report.

BADAL: Have you read Joseph Kerman's new book, *Contemplating Music?*

HOGWOOD: Yes, on musicology.

BADAL: In his section on authentic performance, he makes the point that those who play authentic instruments are rarely virtuosi. If this assessment is fair, doesn't this fact color the quality of what is being put out?

HOGWOOD: No! I think that was not a statistically well-based remark, and Joe was writing, I think, on maybe the evidence of the West Coast over the last ten or fifteen years, where, I guess, as anywhere else, there's been a lot of well-meant but premature exposure of experiments. I think the percentage of virtuosi to total people involved in the early music world is at least as high if not, I would estimate, considerably higher than the percentage of virtuosi to the norm in the conventional conservatoire world. There is one Pollini, one Michelangelo for ten thousand concert pianists in the normal concert world, whereas there is one Malcolm Bilson, and one or two other names one can think of, in proportion to something like twenty or twenty-five professional fortepianists in the world.

BADAL: I remember when Eugen Jochum conducted one of our American chamber ensembles in either Mozart or Haydn, at least one critic complained that American groups seem to feel that rhythm in that repertoire must be treated very rigidly.

HOGWOOD: Oh, yes. I think everybody knits his own authenticity, and what is in fashion now is obviously not going to be in fashion in twenty years' time. So I would give no greater kudos to the current work in recording. It's not a contribution forever. It is a symptom of the state of mind and competence and ambitions of certain individuals at the moment, and the fact that some happen to have taken on a platform of historical awareness with historical instruments is no different than a jazz player who has taken on a particular style of improvising or a symphony orchestra which has taken on a particular music director and a particular way of exploiting scores of Schubert or Berlioz or Bartók or whomever. People listen nowadays to what Mengelberg did with the Concertgebouw or what Neville Marriner did with the Academy of St. Martin's or what "authentic performance," in quotes, did ten or fifteen years ago. I listen to things we did ourselves, and I blush to think that we thought this was the last word. It wasn't. It was the first and only word available in 1973 on that particular line of thought, and it stands no more elevated than that.

BADAL: Our conception of what an authentic performance is seems to have changed radically in the last couple of years. I can remember twenty years ago when Karl Richter was looked upon as the last word in Bach scholarship. Today, he is regarded as very old fashioned—someone on the right track, but only two or three notches above Leopold Stokowski.

HOGWOOD: But highly musical! I think that's one of the first tests. Authenticity is a shorthand for a number of concepts, some of which have come to the front, I think, only in the last ten years or so. The thought of original instruments carries favor for some people, you know, real anguish to others, and what one is encouraging all along the way is a distinction of vocabulary. Richter was playing Bach to people on perfectly modern instruments, but in a way that did not make it sound as though they could, with equal ease, have been playing Tchaikovsky. He made a distinction between the Romantic repertoire and the Baroque repertoire.

BADAL: Do you think the existence of records aids in the evolution of our conceptions?

HOGWOOD: It seems to speed it because more people hear your experiment within the first year who previously would have to wait perhaps five years to hear it in the flesh. So records are a sort of visiting card, and they do announce your experimental intentions or discoveries to a lot of people who may or may not accept them. I think the fact that symphony orchestras in America, for instance, have increasingly shown an interest over the last ten years or so in developing a vocabulary and style suitable to earlier periods without changing their basic instruments is very much related to the fact that the members of these orchestras and their publics have heard the results of these experiments, probably from Europe, and have decided that the change in vocabulary is important.

BADAL: Isn't it a little more difficult to realize that change of vocabulary on a modern instrument? A friend of mine who is a pianist said that when he first played Bach on a harpsichord, it seemed so easy. All the problems he faced when playing Bach on a piano disappeared when he played on a harpsichord.

HOGWOOD: One has a problem of limitation. I would hate to say things suddenly become easy when you play them on the right instrument; but you certainly know that the success, your success, at following the indications in the musical shorthand that the composer leaves you is more assured, because at least he was writing signs on paper that related to the mechanisms and sounds that you have in front of you. There is no way that Bach could have given you suitable marks on a page for interpretation on a Steinway grand.

BADAL: That's another point that Kerman makes, that even playing Beethoven on a contemporary piano produces problems.

HOGWOOD: Exactly! Well, I mean, even playing Debussy on a contemporary piano or Chopin is a very different affair from what they had in mind. We are going to have twentieth-century ears whatever is done by way of performance. We have heard Stravinsky, and there is no way we are not going to hear Stravinsky. Therefore, all the Bach we listen to is with post-Stravinsky ears; but I think there is a great virtue in giving, for instance, Bach credit for being a great man, not only in terms of how he composed but in his ability to deal with material available to him. You don't despise Rembrandt for using the painting materials of his time. You don't wish that he had acrylics and fluorescent paints. He worked ideally within the natural limitations of the materials available, and it's this working within specified limits, like writing a sonnet in fourteen lines, that's important. Things aren't helped by expanding the sonnet to 150 lines. You don't get a better sonnet; you get a different poem. I don't think there is essentially anything gained by according Bach all the later, the post–Industrial Revolution aspects of instrument technology because he was writing within a circumscribed area, and he wanted to use that full field. Mozart wrote concerti for a piano which he himself describes as a perfect instrument. One mustn't weep and regret that poor Mozart didn't have a Steinway grand, because he tells us exactly the opposite. He was very happy with what he had. But he did use it to its full. He used its lowest note and its highest note frequently. I don't know when the last time was that any one pianist has had to use the very bottom note of a Steinway or the very top note, but you could safely cover an octave at either end of the modern grand and nobody would be any worse off. It seems to me that the mechanism has run away from the actual musical requirement.

BADAL: Did recordings play any role in your early musical education?

HOGWOOD: Yes. I now regard recordings more as a library for reference than as a source of pleasure. I'm a little bit biased in this, in that I spent twelve years doing a weekly one-hour program for the BBC that was run on recorded music, taking all sorts of themes for talks which I very much enjoyed doing; but it did force one to listen to an extraordinary number of records per week, often just to find out how long they lasted. You'd discover they lasted a little bit too long, so you couldn't use them on the program. So in fact I rather supersaturated myself with recorded experience.

Now, I will buy recordings as reference. I would like to know what Simon Rattle was doing with his last Janáček, his last Sibelius, whatever; I will listen to it once, then stash it away, and maybe run for it some other time when I want it as reference. But I will rarely settle down to a recorded program, as it were, for an evening's entertainment. What I will do very frequently, more and more frequently now, is use recordings as musical examples in the course of conversation when people are at my home. I particularly call on more and more early recordings: for instance, play Elgar conducting his own Cello Concerto if you want to talk to people about why authentic performance means more than Bach. It's within living memory. Early Stravinsky recordings as opposed to late Stravinsky! The transfers of someone like Moritz Rosenthal, pupil of Liszt, playing on piano roles, now transferred to records via the medium of the perfectly modern, unembarrassingly grand piano. Fantastic!

BADAL: Or Emil Sauer playing the two Liszt concerti!

HOGWOOD: That's right, that's right! I'm just working on the Grieg Piano Concerto to do with the L.A. Philharmonic. I've been working through the two recordings of Percy Grainger, who Grieg said played the concerto better than anybody he ever knew. You have two recordings made by Grainger late in his life, one with Stokowski, and the very early piano role recordings of him playing the cadenza as a sort of control on what the late recordings contain. By pooling all of these, you can begin to see what was consistent, what was intended, what his performing style in this piece was. There's a vast difference from the way that piece is treated nowadays. All this should be used as a model, together with the model edition he made for Schirmer's of that piece, to institute a sense of historical propriety about an old warhorse. But on the whole, the idea of approaching an orchestra or a pianist with any philosophy of treating the Grieg Concerto as an historical piece requiring musicology is unheard of.

BADAL: You raise an interesting point. The authentic performance movement seems to have worked its way up through early Beethoven and then stopped. You'll have a scholar somewhere sweating over a Bach manuscript trying to figure out what Bach intended, yet he will show no interest in a recording of Furtwängler conducting a Bruckner symphony—a man born into the age when that music was new.

HOGWOOD: Yes, I must say I agree with you that it has worked forward from the Renaissance and Baroque eras. Scholarship, Germanic scholarship, was very medieval- and Renaissance-based for a long time, and it has gradually moved forward chronologically. I don't have any feeling that they've stopped. I mean, it was only a little while ago it was unheard of to think of playing Mozart on anything other than modern instruments, but Bach was OK. Fine! You could play Bach on the harpsichord, but the idea of a Steinway piano for Mozart, even his own Steinway piano, was out of the question. Who would dream of playing Mozart on anything other than a Steinway? Now things have changed. I've made records of Mendelssohn and Schubert on original instruments. I think authentic performance is an ongoing interest. There's a magazine been founded, *Nineteenth Century Music*, which examines these questions. The repertoire is there; the public knows it; the musicologists are working on it. And you get occasional articles, like in *Music and Letters* last year, analyzing where string players who played for Brahms were inclined to put vibrato when playing the piano quartet or the Piano Quintet. This was analyzed, and it was a very interesting thing. And it relies suddenly on recorded evidence from the beginning of the century. But I don't think there's a dead end. I think there's maybe a feeling that before we launch too firmly into the nineteenth century with rules and regulations and pronouncements, we have got to digest an enormous amount of information.

BADAL: Of course, the nineteenth century would be the wrong place for rules and regulations per se.

HOGWOOD: No! I think in terms of history you can as easily analyze the nineteenth as you can the fourteenth.

BADAL: Isn't the performance of the music of any age something like the study of linguistics? Linguistic theory says that there is no right or wrong, there is only what the majority of the people do at a given time.

HOGWOOD: Yes, that's the French Academy view; but there is good grammar and bad grammar. There is even more so, not only in linguistics but in literature, the general question of communication or noncommunication. If you begin to use words in such a way that they mean nothing to the people hearing these words, you have failed as a communicator; and then very shortly afterwards, I think linguistics will prove you wrong, too. I think there is a right and wrong, but then there is also stylish usage and unstylish usage. These things change, but they are very much the symptoms of a growing vocabulary and a feeling of the application of fashion to art, which is very important. Art has abstract standards, and fashion has definable moods, and I think it's the interface of these two that gives you, in any period, the individual voice of the creator first and then the power of a group, a movement, a school, a nationality, a style. One knows perfectly well that Vienna is never going to be the same as Berlin, and Berlin is never going to be the same as Moscow, and none of them the same as New York. There is a language always appropriate to their art which will reflect many things symptomatic of that particular spot in time. What I find very upsetting is that, despite the congruence of all these particular disciplines at one time which makes the development of an art a possibility, if you miss out on one or two of these ingredients, then that art might never have taken place. If you had not had a Christian religion, there would be a great blank where we now find this enormous corpus of early church music. If you end up with a period which is only five percent Christian, as nowadays, you have to reestablish some sort of feeling that a cathedral building was conceived of as the right place for the performance of certain repertoire, and therefore the acoustics of that building, whether or not you believe in its religious tenets, are implicit in that music and its performance.

BADAL: The Berlioz Requiem, for example.

HOGWOOD: The Berlioz Requiem is of a scale and size that only suits certain buildings. You are under an obligation not only to play the notes he wrote but, I think, to assemble the instruments he intended and the acoustics he had in mind. This is all council of perfection.

BADAL: Do you find historical performances of Baroque repertoire on records interesting? Is there anything to be learned from Schweitzer and Landowska playing Bach or from Mengelberg and Furtwängler performing the *St. Matthew Passion?*

HOGWOOD: Absolutely, yes. I love listening to them as a musician, and speaking as a harpsichordist, of course, I wouldn't be here if Landowska hadn't existed, so there's a certain reverence there. Speaking as an historian, I am obviously more interested the closer the recorded document is to the original creation. Therefore, if I can hear somebody playing on record who did play for Brahms, and he is playing Brahms's music, I rate that very high as an historical document. If that same person then plays the Bach Chaconne, well I know he never met Bach and in fact is quite a long way away from the Bach ideal as we have established it by other forms of back-bearing on this problem. It therefore doesn't rank so high as an historical document; it may rank very high as a musical document. But I think if you have firsthand source material—I mean, we have Stravinsky conducting his own works on record.

BADAL: Unfortunately, most of the ones that survive are the later recordings.

HOGWOOD: Some, yes. But I think it is now valid to use these recordings as in the past you would have used a later, corrected manuscript from Mozart. If he wrote three versions of a piece, you would take the last written version and say, "This is valid evidence for what he intended." With Stravinsky you find he sometimes changed speeds, dynamics, even notes in the recordings that never got back into print. There are several works, of course, which are riddled with misprints anyway, and the only way of checking what he really meant is to hear what he recorded—just because he never went back and corrected the printed version. I found doing *Dumbarton Oaks* an awful lot of omissions in that piece. And misconceptions and curious misreadings have occurred which can be put right, partly by studying the original—which doesn't seem to have been looked at closely for quite a long while—and partly by consulting the recordings where Stravinsky does go back on some of the things which are in print.

BADAL: Music is an art that exists in time. If you were to conduct the same piece twice in a row, the second performance would be different from the first. I am tempted to think that Baroque music, which relies so much on improvisation and ornamentation, may be aesthetically less suited to phonographic reproduction than something like a Brahms symphony, because at least the score of a Brahms symphony is set; there is no improvisation.

HOGWOOD: Yes, I quite agree. I think as a philosophical question it's absolutely valid. Music was not meant to be trapped in time and repeated exactly, and therefore we are doing something unnatural and only available through twentieth-century technology. I noticed somebody very recently suggested in print that the follow-up to the compact disc was going to be the variable recording with a sort of random selection mechanism inside, and the disc would actually contain seven or eight performances, amongst which the random selector would jump, so that you might never get the same performance of the second subject as you'd had of the first subject. I think it is, to my mind, only a practical problem, since recording is, as I say, a photograph of an event, and sure, the event would take place differently the next day. But recordings will restrain you in certain ways. You put your finger on things like improvisation and embellishment and so on. I personally try to restrain all the people who work with me when we record, and the performances we put on disc will tend to go for the lower end of the scale of exuberance.

BADAL: Might that be because it will repeat more effectively more often?

HOGWOOD: Yes! If you take these wild risks and do a fantastic cadenza in a live performance, the audience will stand and cheer, and you will think, "Thank goodness that worked! What a marvelous thing!" If you hear it twenty-five times in succession on a disc, it begins to lose its effect. Or even worse, I think it begins to color your memory of the piece; so the next time you hear somebody doing it, you sense a lack of that particular cadenza which you've grown used to. So I think it's best to be minimal about your additions, to be restrained. I'm often criticized for being rather laid back and cool and precise in recordings but not often in live performances, because I will allow performances to take their head much more than I would allow a recording to take its head and then embarrass us for another twenty years.

BADAL: Let me ask you a very practical question. In your book *Handel,* you point out that the orchestration of his *Messiah* changed from the Dublin premiere to the first performance in London and that much of the score exists in several different variants. And of course, there is always the ongoing debate over how big or how small the performing apparatus should be. When you made your recording of *Messiah,* how did you decide exactly what you were going to record?

HOGWOOD: One's ambition should be, at least in my mind, not to produce a mongrel that never existed. Handel wrote the piece, and it stands, together with many eighteenth-century pieces, as a popular work that turned up again and again, each time taking a different turning according to the geography that year: availability of singers, place, money, all the rest of it. You can define these fairly closely. The *Messiah* went, in Handel's mind, through a number of stages, most of them documentable, and you can fairly easily say, "I am giving, as far as historical evidence will allow me, a representation of the first performance in Dublin, the first London performance, the performance of 1745, of 1749." The edition I made for Neville Marriner several years back was based on the first London version; therefore, certain pieces were in, certain other pieces were out. The version I did with my own orchestra for L'Oiseau-Lyre was based on the version left with the Foundling Hospital in Handel's will—so therefore the last performing material which he left behind.

BADAL: Why did you pick that one?

HOGWOOD: I picked that because it is well documented. Not only do we have the score and the individual parts, but we have the account books, the checkbooks that tell you how many people were paid and how much they were paid. We know how many violins were paid, how many violas, how many oboes. You find, mysteriously, they paid for two horns. What did they play? They didn't pay them for nothing, I'm quite sure. They could have been used for interval bells. It was a very normal thing in the eighteenth century to summon the audience back after the interval with a horn fanfare. It was also normal eighteenth-century practice when you had horns to double the trumpets the octave lower, which is what we in fact did on the recording.

BADAL: I read recently, and it rather surprised me, that Georg Solti consulted with you before he made his recording of *Messiah.* Is that true?

HOGWOOD: Yes! We had long talks about this. He was very interested in what musicology had to offer, how it could solve practical problems, and to what extent you could disregard it. I was to a certain extent of the mind that if you are working with perfectly modern orchestra and chorus, it would be very nice to see the revival of a non-Handelian version: the Beecham-Goosens version or Sir Michael Costa's—some of these things that we don't know about. But on the other hand, that could rather fracture some of the most important elements in the piece.

BADAL: I remember that Beecham-Goosens *Messiah.*

HOGWOOD: It's a very impressive bit of orchestration, and so long as it's not pretending to be Handel, I'm very happy with it. I haven't heard the result of the Solti recording, but the conversations with him, I found, were fascinating. His insight into the problems and the questions that had immediately struck him about the score were very valid, and to tell the truth, some of them cannot be answered by musicology. They are still open questions of performance and style, and have to be solved individually. I mean, we don't have chapter and verse for the half of the things people imagine musicologists have answers for. A lot of it, I'm glad to say, still relies on personal taste, ability, and artistry.

BADAL: I can't imagine two people of such differing traditions conducting the *Messiah* as you and Georg Solti. I remember thinking something similar when you were recording the Mozart symphonies, because if I remember correctly, at that time the only other complete set was Karl Böhm's. What do they bring—Böhm to Mozart, Solti to Handel—that's different from what you would bring?

HOGWOOD: Well, obviously the weight of a long tradition of something. As I said, I haven't heard the Solti recording. The Böhm recordings of Mozart, which I know, are the result of a very long tradition of playing styles and Böhm's approach to music in general. It's a personal vocabulary. Bruno Walter did the same. You deduce it rather more clearly in the case of Bruno Walter from the recordings of rehearsals that he left. You hear him doing the "Linz" Symphony and how he put the Bruno Walter mark on those particular notes. I'm fascinated by all that sort of evidence, because it shows how malleable music is. But one thing which is obviously lacking by definition in the recent early music revival is tradition. We are always working on new stuff. I'm in the middle of recording the Beethoven symphonies.

BADAL: I didn't know that.

HOGWOOD: I think the First and Second come out this year sometime, and I shall be home in a month or so doing the "Eroica."

BADAL: Are these going to be authentic?

HOGWOOD: They will be with all Beethoven instruments, corrected texts, and everything else. Beethoven is the cutting edge for the moment of this sort of experiment. I think it will be very interesting. I hope it will be a catalyst to a lot of similar experiments. But one cannot bring to bear the weight of a lifetime's experience of performing the "Eroica" in this style, which is what you get from the majority of other recordings, because it doesn't exist.

BADAL: Since our conceptions of performing Beethoven still tend to be rather late-nineteenth century, it will be very interesting to see how these will be received.

HOGWOOD: Yes! Well, there's still a shudder in some quarters when one mentions Beethoven in this context, as there was when we first mentioned Mozart five years ago. And when we've done Beethoven and Schubert symphonies, the next candidate is obviously the Berlioz *Symphonie fantastique*. People shudder at that: authentic Berlioz? But he wrote a whole book on orchestration. He very explicitly understood the capacities and capabilities of each of those instruments as they existed in the 1820s.

BADAL: You seem to favor a chronological approach.

HOGWOOD: Yes! We found it worked very well with Mozart. When we hit the "Jupiter" Symphony, it was the last Mozart symphony we played, and we had the experience of going through all the discoveries of the earlier symphonies, which is something akin to how Mozart's own players must have worked. Many of them were Baroque musicians.

BADAL: Wouldn't there be a further practical consideration? Few know those early symphonies.

HOGWOOD: We certainly didn't.

BADAL: Wouldn't you encounter less resistance to your approach from the public by beginning with the earlier symphonies?

HOGWOOD: I don't think I feel very bound in to what people are used to anyway. When it's built into the musicians, then it's a different question. If you work with musicians with no going authentic vocabulary, only the traditional approach, and you start on a traditional symphony such as the "Jupiter" or the G Minor, then the danger is that the discoveries you might have made in Mozart phraseology by starting on less well known works without this inbred tradition will be missed, because you will fall into just the way that is familiar, already in your mind's ear. So I think it's logical to go for the "unsolid" repertoire first and move forwards. But you can't avoid the problem with Beethoven. My orchestra and I come to Beethoven with a repertoire of devices deduced from the workings of Mozart and Haydn and limited, to a certain extent, by our experience with Schubert as a sort of control on the other end. But the field in between, the last of the Haydns and the first of the Schuberts, is entirely uncharted. Yet the sounds of those symphonies are very familiar to everyone in their traditional versions. What tends to immediately shock everyone, of course, is any suggestion that, for example, the Beethoven metronome might have been right. You say to yourself, "Right, play the finale at the speed he marked!" And then, to your surprise, you find that, with the size band that he used and the instruments that we have, it's possible to do it. It is not unmusical. It is certainly fast. But we assume his players could play it, and it's a challenge to us to play it as well.

BADAL: How do you feel about digital sound?

HOGWOOD: I'm not a hi-fi person. I'm almost anti-hi-fi, to the despair of engineers and so on, but I am very impressed by the later developments like the compact disc. That seems to be a major easing of the transition from the actual sounds the musicians make to the ears of the consumer.

BADAL: Won't technology, to a certain extent, determine which performances will survive? Böhm recorded some of the later Mozart symphonies with the Vienna Philharmonic after the Berlin Philharmonic set had been completed. They are not as good as the ones in the Berlin set, but they will probably survive because they are newer.

HOGWOOD: Well, not necessarily. I think in that case what a man is often doing is laying down the groundwork of his own biography. What you have from these people is a point-by-point description of their own powers and their own views on music through their lives. I love the idea that people record the same piece three or four times. I mean, Brendel has covered the same ground quite a few times, as have Harnoncourt and Karajan. You can pick up, you know, three different recordings of the Brandenburgs from Harnoncourt with ten years between each, and they're fascinating documents. I don't think it's so much based on which is better or worse any more than we can say nowadays which is the better pyramid or which is the worse pyramid. The fact that the Pyramids were built at all and have survived gives us remarkable insight into that period—its achievements, its ambitions, its technology.

BADAL: Are you comfortable in the recording studio?

HOGWOOD: I love the recording studio, yes.

BADAL: There are some musicians who are not.

HOGWOOD: Sure, I know! There are some, of course, like Glenn Gould, who are almost more comfortable there than at a public concert. This is a matter of temperament. But I regard it as a laboratory, and I'm very grateful to be given so well-equipped a laboratory so frequently to work on material which one knows at the start is of such value. You are using the medium as something different from your live performance. One of the things you can do with it is play greater experiments. Try this, that, and the other! Assemble companies of instruments that would never be seen in a live performance! I mean, a museum will maybe part with a rare instrument for two or three days to make a recording which they would never, never let you take on a concert tour or leave the country with. So I can record with original eighteenth-century instruments something I could never perform on a concert with those same instruments. I therefore will seize my opportunity in a three-hour session and say, "Here for the first, perhaps last time, I have a whole set of eighteenth-century oboes, bassoons, and a contrabassoon, the one that Handel actually saw and heard." I shall make sure that I don't just do one through-take of the piece with the contra and leave it at that, but I will experiment with the contra in various octaves, various placements, various styles, to make sure I have got the most out of that particular experiment. In retrospect, I will then decide what fits the bill best in terms of the whole performance. But the outtakes are not necessarily disgraces; they are discarded experiments. I find the recording environment is, in fact, a very creative one.

BADAL: I suppose there are not many recording companies that would willingly pay you for your experimentation.

HOGWOOD: Well, I'm not sure it is, as you imply, wasteful.

BADAL: From my point of view it's not wasteful, but there must be somebody who is simply looking at the bottom line.

HOGWOOD: Well, no! We actually get onto tape as much as the Academy of St. Martin's, which is certainly not an experimental orchestra, gets onto tape. We get the twelve to fifteen minutes' worth of finished music, plus the experiments out of a three-hour English recording session. What I don't have to do with these players is debate style and so on. I mean, with a modern orchestra I have to put in all the trills for them. I never have to waste time with that with stylistic players, because it's second nature. They speak the language. So I can then go on to another stage of experimentation—time which might have been used on some other kind of experiment with a modern orchestra.

BADAL: Would you call yourself an adherent to the principle of the long take?

HOGWOOD: Yes! Of course, having covered the repertoire that we have covered, there are not many pieces that will even last twenty minutes. But, yes, one gives performances. However, I am not in the least bit embarrassed, in fact I'm very intrigued, by the power of the engineer and the editor to splice and edit, especially when there is, as Joe Kerman rather rudely suggests, an audible incompetence on the part of the player that has to be overcome with the razor blade. But unless there is an audible musical deficiency in something put together, I no more object to an edited record than I object to an edited film. Nobody imagines they're going to the cinema to see a straight shoot. It is edited.

BADAL: Media theorists say that people tend to accept the level of technology they are born into but regard succeeding developments as dangerous. Do you see any danger from the increased application of technology to music?

HOGWOOD: I must say that, treated with the right philosophical outlook, which is "The music comes first, the technology second," I see no danger whatsoever. I think technology is a wonderful implement to have. I wouldn't agree with the theorists there. There was no feeling on the part of the early pianists, like Mozart and Beethoven, that the piano they began with was the ultimate and that every later piano was a threat; it was quite the reverse. They wanted the technical improvements because they wanted to speak a language that was developing. And so every note that was added to the range of the keyboard, every new mechanical device put there, they utilized. They didn't backspace and say that an improved piano was what was required for their earlier music; they related to the state of the art as it developed. But there was no threat; there was an expanding horizon. I see exactly the same happening in the electronic media. I mean, one knows perfectly well that digital recording is encoding far more information about a musical performance than can yet be reproduced by the present state of loudspeakers. So the capturing is, at the moment, ahead of the reproduction, and I look forward to the march of progress in reproduction over the next twenty years which will increasingly bring more and more to my ears out of those compact discs. The fact that compact discs are not indestructible but a great deal less prone to destruction than previous types of media seems to me, again, no threat whatsoever, but a positive benefit.

BADAL: If we follow your line of thought to its logical or, perhaps, illogical conclusion, don't we arrive at a point where what is coming out of a speaker can never be duplicated at a live concert? In his second book *The Composer's Advocate,* Erich Leinsdorf talks about the man who goes to a live concert and doesn't like it because it doesn't sound like his stereo system.

HOGWOOD: Exactly! You have a lot of people like that, and there are a lot of people who should strictly be defined as hi-fi enthusiasts rather than music enthusiasts. This is not, in any way, the problem of the technology or the musician, I'm glad to say; it's a problem of those doing the listening. There may be people who prefer high-color reproductions of works of art to going to museums to see those works of art. There may originally have been people who felt that the printed book was an insult to the written word. It was true the printed book did not look like the written word. But it wasn't pretending to; it was doing another job. And I think the art and science of recording are quite a different business from the art and science of giving a performance. It is carte blanche, I think, to take the philosophical stance you wish in relation to a musical work. A Mozart symphony belongs to nobody; it mercifully can be killed by nobody, do what you like. The obligation is on you to perform music rather than to shut it away in a bank vault and not look at it. It would be a crime, I think, given the choice between performing music in any way and not performing it, to choose the second course. You have to perform. You may willingly change your style of performance, your objectives in performance, but your relationship is always primarily with the composer's evidence and, to my mind, also with the historical evidence. After that, you go through a number of chambers controlled by different magicians en route to the listener. One of these particular magicians is, of course, the media man. But he's only one chamber. I think we want the true word to come through as clearly as possible from the original creator to the individual ear.

VLADIMIR ASHKENAZY

✧

PIANIST VLADIMIR ASHKENAZY took up the baton rather late in his career. He therefore shares with colleague and friend Daniel Barenboim the rather unusual distinction of having recorded portions of the concerto literature first as soloist and later as conductor. Both also released competing sets of the Beethoven piano concerti, playing and conducting from the keyboard.

Although hardly an unknown quantity when he turned to conducting, Ashkenazy and London Records faced the same repertoire problems that plague any younger maestro trying to establish a reputation through work in the studio. The Russian repertoire seemed an obvious choice; and Ashkenazy has made some notable recordings of Rachmaninov, Shostakovich, and Prokofiev, the complete rendition of the latter's ballet *Cinderella* with the Cleveland Orchestra proving especially impressive.

Other choices, however, seemed more questionable. The quality of the interpretations is really not the issue, and one can admire Ashkenazy's courage for facing the competition—heavy in collections of Strauss tone poems and Debussy-Ravel orchestral works, ferocious in Beethoven and Brahms symphonies. Given the extraordinary glut in these areas of the repertoire, however, will the same audience that buys him playing Brahms on the piano buy him conducting the same composer from the podium? Perhaps in an effort to give his Brahms symphony cycle some visibility, London has coupled some of the individual symphony recordings with short Dvořák selections rather than the standard Brahms overtures.

I interviewed Vladimir Ashkenazy in July of 1985 during his appearance at Blossom. The ancillary building behind the orchestra pavilion is a sterile, concrete affair, but at least it offers air-conditioned comfort on hot, humid summer days. Ashkenazy, however, opted instead for a lovely pastoral setting under a large tree. ✧

Vladimir Ashkenazy conducts the Cleveland Orchestra. Photo by Peter Hastings.

BADAL: Any conductor your age growing up in the West would have had records available to him as part of his musical education. Did you have records available to you as part of your musical training in the Soviet Union?

ASHKENAZY: Yes, yes! There were many records released, too, but not as many as in the West, and basically oriented to Russian and Soviet music. The LPs came—of course, everything came later than in the West. They don't tend to invent things. They don't seem to be so technologically minded, you see. So the LPs came several years after they did in the West, and stereo came much later than in the West. And, of course, the variety of repertoire was limited, as I already said, and basically oriented to the Russian and Soviet music, with some exceptions, of course. But the lion's share was the indigenous music, which is, in a way, understandable. That presented one of the problems, of course. But I was one of the lucky ones because I traveled to the West, and I bought all the things that I needed in the West, you see. So for me, my record collection was extremely important.

BADAL: Were there any that particularly impressed you?

ASHKENAZY: Oh, there were so many that I couldn't single out one or two. I was very keen on learning new repertoire that we didn't have in Russia.

At that time, for instance, Stravinsky wasn't allowed to be played, you know. So I bought *Petrushka, The Rite of Spring, The Firebird,* and other pieces by Stravinsky. And we couldn't find, for instance, a good recording of Debussy's *La Mer,* or even one at all. As I say, the stress was always on the Russian or Soviet music. So the rest of the repertoire didn't seem to have a lot of variety, and there wasn't much option.

BADAL: Would there be essentially Russian performers as well?

ASHKENAZY: Also yes, at that time. But you know, in the intervening years since I left, the situation has changed, and I think there are more—I think they buy some tapes and release them on Russian records. And sometimes they do pirating you know, and release them on the Soviet label.

BADAL: It works both ways.

ASHKENAZY: It works both ways, of course. So now there is much more variety, both in repertoire and in performers, too. But the main stress is still on the Russian music, I'm sure.

BADAL: Was it much of a shock when you heard Western performance styles?

ASHKENAZY: Yes! I think it was a pleasant shock. Basically, the orchestral playing was on quite a different level altogether—not to be compared with the level of Russian orchestras at that time, except maybe the Leningrad Philharmonic. Even that's a limited orchestra, but a wonderful orchestra.

BADAL: There are some old Mravinsky recordings with the Leningrad Philharmonic that are just wonderful.

ASHKENAZY: Yes, some of them are really very, very good. But the repertoire was very, very limited, and the scope of expression, to my taste, also was limited. But what they did in their area of repertoire, they did very well. It was a very, very good group. Now it's changed a lot, so I don't know what they are like now.

BADAL: There are stories in the West that after World War II, the Russian army took tapes from the Berlin radio archives, and so there are Furtwängler performances available in the Soviet Union that are not available in the West.

ASHKENAZY: I'm not quite sure, because I haven't been back for more than twenty years. Maybe there are some available. When I was there still— that's up till 1963—I remember they did release a few of Furtwängler's records, but those I found in the West as well.[1]

BADAL: Is the historical aspect of recordings very important to you?

ASHKENAZY: Difficult to say! You know, times have changed so much that when I hear—I couldn't say that I don't learn anything when I listen to some performances that were considered great at the time, but I can't say I'm often very enamored of those performances. I can appreciate certain qualities, but I learn more from some of today's performances, basically of the times closer to us. I think, I don't know, the attitude is less affected today, more straight somehow, more to the point, and I like that.

BADAL: I recently heard Oskar Fried's performance of Mahler's Second Symphony, and it's amazing to hear how free the style was.

ASHKENAZY: Oh, that, of course! That was the style then. Much too much! It's quite unnecessary, I think. Music lives without those affectations very well—some phrasings, tempos, and some exaggerations that are quite unnecessary. Music doesn't really need those. That's why I say I very often appreciate certain things like intensity of performance, commitment, and the ability to communicate, but not so often other qualities—other purely musical qualities, you know, like phrasing or tempo, all these unnecessary affectations. These I don't like, really.

BADAL: Do you use recordings professionally?

ASHKENAZY: Yes, I do. When I learn a piece, I usually check myself if I know it well by playing a recording.

BADAL: Since you came to conducting rather late, do you use recordings more than someone who began his career as a conductor?

ASHKENAZY: I wouldn't know. How can I compare? You see, I don't separate myself—conductor or pianist or whatever. I'm a musician. I'm interested in music. I love music. It's my life. And even before I began to conduct, I knew so many performances of so many different pieces. You know, recordings played a very major role in my life, in my interest in music. So now, for instance, maybe I have to learn a symphony that I've heard a few hundred times and have ten versions of at home. I already know what it sounds like. I even remember some performances. So how can you ask me whether I use recordings or not? It's a continuing process. As I say, the way I use recordings now, when I learn a piece, I will play a recording and see whether I really learned it or not—that I haven't omitted something, you know. Once or twice I might listen to a performance that I've listened to before but don't remember very well. I want to see what I thought of it before, what I think of it now. I might incorporate something into my own understanding of the piece; I might reject it completely.

BADAL: Some musicians say that when you use recordings, there's a danger that you'll learn the performance and not the piece of music.

ASHKENAZY: Well, that's why I say that I first learn the piece, and then I play a recording to check whether I know it or not. That doesn't mean I'll conduct it the way I heard it.

BADAL: Many musicians feel that it's dangerous for young musicians to use recordings. Kurt Masur feels that young conductors may imitate what they hear on records, and Erich Leinsdorf says they may even be inclined to do the opposite of what they hear.

ASHKENAZY: I don't know. It depends on the individual. It depends on how strong an idea you have about the piece you're going to perform. If you don't have a strong idea, then you might be influenced. It depends on your character and your degree of commitment, I suppose on the strength of your concept about the piece. And what is the difference between a recording or a live performance? If the same conductor conducted a live performance and a recording, they might be the same; they might not be the same.

BADAL: Do you conduct differently for a recording than for a live performance?

ASHKENAZY: No, I don't think so.

BADAL: The same.

ASHKENAZY: Yes, of course.

BADAL: If you were to conduct the same piece twice in a row, the second performance would be different from the first.

ASHKENAZY: I suppose so.

BADAL: But a recording will always be the same. Some musicians are bothered by that. Does it bother you?

ASHKENAZY: No. Why should it bother me? It's a fact of life. Why should it bother me? We record something, and we try to do our best.

BADAL: Do you like the long take?

ASHKENAZY: Of course. We do a whole piece first, and then see what we need, you know. Imperfections and things like that need to be covered. Symphonies we do movement by movement. If you have to go back to a movement, it's difficult for everybody to get into the atmosphere again.

BADAL: Do you like working in a recording studio?

ASHKENAZY: Very much.

BADAL: Some musicians don't.

ASHKENAZY: Well, it depends on the individual. I've done so much. I don't really think there is any difference between a live performance and a recording. A recording has also to be full of spontaneity.

BADAL: Isn't that harder to achieve in a studio than at a live performance?

ASHKENAZY: Well, if the music doesn't inspire you, then that's your problem, I think. Music has to inspire you, and not the fact that it is a public performance, you see. Otherwise, why are we musicians if we can perform only when there are people listening? In any case, there is an audience, even at a recording session. First of all, there is a producer and a producing team; secondly, usually a couple of friends from the orchestra or whatever. They're quite a few people, usually. In any case, if there is one person listening, still you are playing—even if there is nobody listening, you know eventually someone will be listening to it, to your performance, so you have to give the same degree of communicativeness, so to speak, the same degree of commitment and spontaneity as if you play it for an audience.

BADAL: There was a time when orchestras had very specific national characteristics. That doesn't seem to be quite so true today. I wonder if records played any role in this.

ASHKENAZY: I can't comment on this very much. I still hear very different sounds when I conduct different orchestras. Maybe you are right, but I don't really know to what degree this is correct. I hear the individual sounds, I must confess. The Berlin and Vienna, of course, the Cleveland, the London orchestras, the Concertgebouw. I find them all really quite different. I don't know if I would be able to identify them on recordings, you know; that's not so easy for anyone. But I certainly hear the differences when I conduct. That's for sure.

BADAL: How do you choose the repertoire you record as a conductor?

ASHKENAZY: It depends on the record company, plans, and on what is salable—you know, on the market, and so on. We simply discuss it and come to a decision that is mutually acceptable.

BADAL: Younger conductors seem to avoid recording certain pieces in the repertoire, yet fairly early in your career as a conductor you recorded Beethoven symphonies. Were you bothered by the fact that every great conductor has recorded them?

ASHKENAZY: No, not at all. I was only concerned with how well I can do them. That's all! I try everything.

BADAL: You recorded Prokofiev's *Cinderella* with the Cleveland Orchestra, but you only played about half of the score at the concert. When was the rest rehearsed?

ASHKENAZY: It wasn't rehearsed. We just came to record it. We rehearsed each number, I think we just played each number through once to rehearse, then recorded it straight away. It was tough going. I mean, only an orchestra like this can do it.

BADAL: How many sessions were there?

ASHKENAZY: Four sessions!

BADAL: How did they go?

ASHKENAZY: Oh, fantastic! I mean, it couldn't go faster than that. It's possible only with an orchestra like this that has no problems in handling the materials, you see. I mean, whatever is there in front of them, they play straight away. That's really quite miraculous.

BADAL: I heard a rumor that London was so pleased with the results that they were actually thinking of recording the complete *Romeo and Juliet* with you and the Cleveland Orchestra. Is there any truth to that rumor?

ASHKENAZY: Oh, yes. They said that, but they have done it with Lorin Maazel. I'll be very pleased to do it, of course, and they know it very well.[2] It should be done maybe in three sessions! I'm joking! I don't know how long.

BADAL: Of course, the orchestra knows it better.

ASHKENAZY: Yes. Still, it's all difficult, but it's a great piece. But we are doing now *Don Quixote* tomorrow. We are recording *La Mer*—a Debussy record in April, so we have good plans. I don't know what happens after that.

BADAL: How do you feel about digital sound? Do you like it?

ASHKENAZY: Yes.

BADAL: There are a lot of people who don't. They say it's unmusical.

ASHKENAZY: No. I don't know what they mean. I think they confuse the issues, basically.

BADAL: What issues?

ASHKENAZY: The issue of faithful reproduction and the issue of how record companies record the material. You see, the fact that digital recording and the compact disc reproduce so faithfully has nothing to do with being unmusical. It's just something to do with reproduction. That's all.

BADAL: It's sometimes possible to hear things on recordings that you could not hear in the concert hall. In his book *The Composer's Advocate,* Erich Leinsdorf talks about someone who listens to a lot of records, then goes to a live concert and doesn't like it because it doesn't sound like his stereo.

ASHKENAZY: Well, that's silly! I usually listen to music. I don't necessarily listen to all the, how can I say, hi-fi details, like I must hear some low frequency in the double basses or in the tuba, or hear some inner voice that might be rather lost in a concert performance. Well, it's a pity if something important is lost in a concert performance, but the main thing is music, and not some sonority that may be nice to hear but if it isn't there it won't really have any great bearing on the performance. That's what we tend to forget. And, you know, hi-fi buffs can be unmusical themselves, actually. And again, to say that faithful reproduction is unmusical in itself is rather unintelligent, I think. What is important is what the performance is like. You see, record companies tend to try to give the record-buying public as good a reproduction as possible. Sometimes it goes into a—well, with some companies it goes into a clinical reproduction. With some other companies, it doesn't go quite that far. The sound has quite a lot of air, reverberation, and space. But they still try to give you on the record what is sometimes impossible in the concert hall. Sometimes, in a way, they enhance things that are difficult to produce in a concert hall. Sometimes they even help the composer himself, who might have misjudged the sonority of the orchestra, the balance, the instrumentation, and there are numerous cases like that. In which case, a recording can be beneficial, actually. You hear what should be heard and what cannot be heard in a concert hall. You see, there are so many aspects to it. But the main thing is the performance itself. You know, I'm not a hi-fi buff because it's not really that important to me: how many voices I'll hear, how many low or high frequencies I'll hear. What is important to me is the direction of the performance, what it has to communicate, you see. And that's not to say that I'll be very pleased if the recording is technically terrible.

BADAL: What do you listen for when you listen to playbacks of your recordings?

ASHKENAZY: I listen to music, basically: the way it goes, whether I've managed to communicate what I want to communicate.

BADAL: If you're faced with two different takes of the same passage, and one is note-perfect and the other contains blemishes but also communicates the spirit more effectively, which one will you choose?

ASHKENAZY: This depends on the degree of the blemishes, you see. Without examples the answer will not be really valid, not honest enough. Of course, spirit is the most important thing. When the blemishes are such that it really disturbs you to listen to it, it's no good.

BADAL: Especially when they are repeated over and over.

ASHKENAZY: Especially when they repeat. So one has to be very careful.

BADAL: If someone hits a wrong note during a performance, you may hear it, but then it's gone. The performance goes on.

ASHKENAZY: You may hear it; you may not. But on a recording, you play it a few times, and in the end you would hear it, you know. But it depends. It depends on the degree of the blemish. I sometimes pass things with blemishes that weren't quite so prominent. But, you know, in other cases I would opt for the note-perfect solution, too. It depends. I can't give you a general answer.

BADAL: Do you ever listen to your recordings after they have been released?

ASHKENAZY: No. I get very tense because I relive the whole mess again, and I get very tired listening to it. So I tend not to listen to them unless I have to.

BADAL: Do you ever go back to a recording you made in the past and say to yourself, "If only I had it to do over again, I would do this differently"?

ASHKENAZY: Yes, of course. It happens. Sometimes it happens that I like it. It happens that I don't like it. Difficult!

BADAL: Media theorists say that people tend to accept the level of technology they are born into but regard further development as a threat.

ASHKENAZY: Threat to what?

BADAL: Art, for example. Do you see any danger to music from the increased application of technology?

ASHKENAZY: I can't quite focus really on what people mean by that. What do they mean in practical terms? How does it affect music and art negatively?

BADAL: Some would say, for example, that people will get to know a single recorded performance but will only know the music superficially.

ASHKENAZY: What is to know music well? What's to know music superficially? Doesn't that depend on the individual—how he takes it, how she takes it? It has nothing to do with technology; it's something to do with people.

BADAL: Like the hi-fi fiend who is not even listening to the piece any more. He's listening to the sound of the recording.

ASHKENAZY: Right, exactly! Yes. I'm not interested in such a person, and I think he's not a music lover, in a way; he's a hi-fi lover. But I have faith in music, in the fact that music has a lot to communicate to people, you see. And those who are receptive and responsive to music, I think, will always be responsive to music. If it's in their genes, you know, their makeup, so to speak, they will respond, and it will depend on them rather than anything else how they react to new technological developments, you know. I love music so much. For me it was like a miracle, you know—especially in my situation in the Soviet Union—that I could get, when I went to the West, recordings of pieces that were very seldom played or almost never played, and I could enjoy them so much, simply emotionally enjoy them, and also get to know music that I couldn't otherwise get to know. So for me it was both educational and incredibly enjoyable, and I believe if people are as committed to music as I was and am—and there are many like that, of course—then that's what they get from records.

BADAL: Education and enjoyment.

ASHKENAZY: Yes! Terrific! I think it's irreplaceable, and I'm very grateful to technology for the invention of recordings and for the fact that it brought recordings to a very high level.

Notes

1. Russian troops took tapes from the radio archives in Berlin. The tapes were ultimately returned to the West in the late 1980s and subsequently issued on compact disc by Deutsche Grammophon. Although some of these performances had circulated commercially and privately in the West before the original copies were returned, the sound was vastly inferior to that of the Berlin tapes.

2. Whether planned or not, the recording never took place.

Part of London's recording setup at Severance Hall. "And I think it's going to be one of the best places to record." —Christoph von Dohnányi. Photos by Denise Blanda.

The removable platform London constructed in the auditorium of Severance Hall for recording sessions. Photos by Denise Blanda.

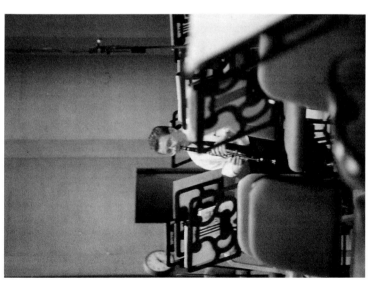

Warming up in Severance Hall before a London session for Bruckner's Symphony No. 7 in August 1990. Photos by Denise Blanda.

Exploring the mysteries of Bruckner's Symphony No. 7 before a recording session in August 1990. Photos by Denise Blanda.

RICCARDO CHAILLY

꒰

RICCARDO CHAILLY has always been an exclusive London artist, and his career in the studio demonstrates a variety of techniques an enterprising label may employ to establish name recognition for a young musician. A well-chosen series of some sort always guarantees a certain amount of visibility; Chailly's Stravinsky recordings included such items as *Renard, Le Chant du rossignol,* and *The Rake's Progress,* the first commercial recording the opera received after the composer's own. He has also fruitfully explored the fringes of the repertoire, notably some of the virtually unknown orchestral compositions of Alexander von Zemlinsky, such as *The Mermaid* and the Symphony in B-Flat.

In a far riskier move, he recorded a number of Bruckner symphonies, making him one of the first non–Northern Europeans, and certainly the first young Italian, to tackle the composer on disc, and placing him in direct competition with such legendary Brucknerians as Furtwängler, Jochum, and Karajan. At the time of our conversation, only Symphony No. 7 had appeared. Though other symphonies followed, as he remarks during the interview, a complete cycle had not been contemplated.

When Chailly appeared with the Cleveland Orchestra in November 1985, his schedule called for him to record Prokofiev's *Alexander Nevsky* following the concert performances. Hence, recording producer Paul Meyers sat in on the interview, along with the maestro's wife. ꒰

BADAL: Maestro, I've talked with a number of major conductors about recordings, and most of them are at least a little ambivalent about them. I've found, however, that younger musicians seem to accept them much more readily. Is this true in your case?

CHAILLY: Personally, I must say I've been a fanatic about records since I was a child. Since I was a very, very young student, I was spending all of my

Riccardo Chailly conducts the Cleveland Orchestra. Photo by Peter Hastings.

little money on records. So I was a fanatic for records—dreaming maybe one day to be a musician and maybe dreaming one day to be an exclusive artist for a record company. And I've been tied to records since my youth. And I believe in records very much, so much that I'm actually one of the few that at the moment is against those who believe that the best way to do a recording is to do a record live. I am against that idea for several reasons. First of all, whoever buys a compact disc today has to face a high price. That's the reality of the situation. And due to the fact that the buyer must pay such a high price, he has the right to expect the best quality and the best—that the performance be next to perfection. We can certainly never be perfect, any artist, but we should try to do our best to be as near perfection as possible. And this you can do only through a studio recording. I don't believe either what for many years people have been saying, "Of course, the feeling! The feeling of a performance, the feeling of a live performance is something akin to—"

BADAL: Of course, some musicians do very well in a recording studio. But Leonard Bernstein, for example, feels he does better at a live concert.

CHAILLY: I tell you! I know that very often the best results come out in the recording studio—more than the live performance. This is absolutely true. The result is that I am against live recordings because they might bring you the feeling, might bring you the main line, but that's generally all that you get. You need to have much more perfection when you listen to perfect sound like on a compact disc.

BADAL: I'm thinking of tapes of live Furtwängler performances which will just knock you out the first time you play them but they don't wear so well. It's the recordings he made in the studio that are easier to live with.

CHAILLY: Let's take—I adore Furtwängler anyway, so—the live recording of the Bruckner Seventh in Cairo with the Berlin Philharmonic on tour. This is an example of perfection. Although the sound is very dry and does not please as you would like, the perfection of the performance is pretty remarkable. It is really a miracle. But this, I would say, is an exception, you know. And generally speaking, when you listen, for instance, to the famous *La Traviata* from La Scala conducted by Giulini . . . . Everybody was dreaming about this historic, unique *Traviata*. My father was there at that famous premiere. You know, I am Milanese, so I know what I am talking about. Listen to it today with ears used to listening to perfection! The ensemble and so on! It sounds extremely messy, and it should be like this because a live performance brings you that. And although I admire Callas immensely, and she was singing fantastically well, this a record that I am not able to listen to with great enjoyment today. It brings exactly what a live performance does bring you: great emotion, but certainly little perfection.

BADAL: Do you feel comfortable in a recording studio?

CHAILLY: I do feel comfortable. And one of the reasons why I am comfortable is because I have a great team surrounding me. There is also a friendly relationship between me and the management of Decca, and that helps immensely, of course, to make you feel comfortable.

BADAL: You mentioned that you were a record fanatic. I assume then that records played an important role in your musical education.

CHAILLY: Yes, indeed! And I especially like to know what was in the past, being a young conductor. I always like to go back to Furtwängler as much as I can, Toscanini as much as I can, De Sabata. You know De Sabata? Our own Italian genius who recorded so little, unfortunately.

BADAL: The De Sabata *Tosca.* If he had never recorded anything else, he would be remembered as a great conductor.

CHAILLY: Yes, indeed! This is the most popular recording. But now Fonte/ Cetra—you know, the Italian label—is bringing out a full album of De Sabata. Live recordings! And also, of course, there you hear what live recording means, but you have a chance to know what De Sabata was.

BADAL: Now that you are a professional conductor, do you still listen to recordings?

CHAILLY: I listen much less because the time I have available for listening is so restricted now, so little. But when I can, I like to listen, especially to compact discs.

BADAL: Do you listen to your own recordings?

CHAILLY: Nearly never! No. Nearly never. I listen when we are trying to finalize the best combination of takes, but afterwards, I actually never go back to them.

BADAL: Many older musicians warn that there is a danger to young musicians if they listen to too many recordings. They suggest that a young musician may be influenced by what he hears, and if that's the case, he may not develop his own personality.

CHAILLY: There is part reality in this; there is part mental masturbation. It is true a young fellow can be seduced by a fantastic performance. But to know what has been done before your time, to have this fortune and not use it would be stupid and silly. I would say a young conductor behaving that way has a very limited brain. To have the fortune today to have on the market whatever you want! You have the way to know what the greatest conductors in the years before our generation were doing. And not to use such a great—to ignore it just to be faithful to your own idea sounds to me so absolutely limiting. But of course, you should certainly not go to a great recording, listen, and try to imitate or try to copy. But if you find something that really moves you so much and you are really convinced of it, why not use it.

BADAL: Isn't there a danger, though, that if you listen to many different recordings of the same piece, your performance may lack unity?

CHAILLY: It could be. I was speaking, for instance, with someone in the Berlin Radio Symphony where, as you know, I am chief conductor. He always used to say, "Oh, I would like to make a tape of my ideal Bruckner Ninth. That means one movement from Walter, one movement from Furtwängler, transition from Günter Wand, and coda from Von Karajan." This is fun! But in the end, it is not true that a conductor, a performer, a performing artist really does that. At least, this is not true in my case.

. . . Let's talk about a real example of what I mean—a tradition that you feel so involved in that you would like to continue it. De Sabata conducted many times in La Scala *Bolero,* and at the final modulation before the close, where the trombones play portamento *raaAA! raaAA!* he utilized the strings of the La Scala Orchestra to sing while the trombones play, to sing with the voice the portamentos. And this is something that I grew up with in my youth. As you know, my father also was very close to De Sabata because my father was a composer and De Sabata examined all the operas he wrote. So my father had very close rapport with him. I also happen to know all the La Scala players because I was assistant conductor to Claudio Abbado there in the early seventies, and I've heard this tradition reported by many people. I actually heard another conductor doing that piece in La Scala with that tradition. So since I was a child, I have heard *Bolero* in La Scala with that special color. It is something which makes you freeze and makes you frightened because it sounds like something is shaking the hall. You don't know where this is coming from, but it is something which will shake you very much indeed. Sixty people are singing, you know, and it's an incredible effect. And I cannot think of doing the *Bolero* without bringing that tradition to it. So when I do the *Bolero* around the world, I always shock the orchestra in the first morning by asking them to do that. But it sounds so moving, that moment, and not cheap because it is a fantastic effect. The piece is in a state of delirium by that time, and this tradition adds something, I would say, extra—I don't know how to say it in English—something untouchable, something indescribable.

BADAL: It seems to me that when younger conductors begin making records, they avoid certain pieces such as Beethoven symphonies and concentrate on pieces which are not so well known. I remember when you started to record, you made a record of Puccini orchestral music, most of it completely unknown.

CHAILLY: You have Paul Myers in this room, and I'm happy to say that he agrees. Now, I am certainly one of those who like to go slowly when approaching a masterpiece: perform it and perform it again, think it and rethink it, but not to go straight to recording. Paul, for instance, was one of the first persons who was so convinced of my promise some years ago when I did the Brahms Fourth Symphony, that he came to me and asked me to start recording it. And I said, "No, Paul! I thank you very much, I appreciate your enthusiasm, but I would like to wait many years—not several, *many* years—to start recording." So I had the chance. I made the choice and asked him to wait, and he understood the reasons and did nothing to push the thing. And the Puccini, for instance, was an idea that I always had because, being an Italian, I had conducted nearly all the Puccini operas for many years. And I happened one day to talk to Maestro Karajan in Berlin, and he told me, "I've been told you just finished recording the Puccini complete symphonic music." And I said yes. "I wish I had the idea forty years ago," he said, "because now I am too old and too involved in other things to do that, but I wonder why I never thought of it." And nobody did until Decca proposed this record. And he said, "I'm sure it's going to be a big hit due to the fact that people adore Puccini's music, and there is so little that people don't know in the symphonic field. It's going to be very much appreciated."

BADAL: His symphonic music is almost completely unknown, at least in this country.

CHAILLY: Even in Italy. Even in Italy, it's not that well known. And all the symphonic music is enough to fill just one LP. That's it! That's all, you know. *Gesamte Ausgabe!*

BADAL: The musical scene is much more international than it used to be. Anyone can conduct Beethoven or Brahms. But some composers we still want to link with conductors from the same national background. We want to hear an Italian conduct Rossini; we want to hear a Frenchman conduct Ravel. Yet you recorded the Bruckner Seventh. I looked in the catalogue, and almost every other recording is conducted by someone older than you from Northern Europe. Did you ever wonder how the public would accept a Bruckner Seventh from a young Italian?

CHAILLY: I never asked myself this question because I approach Bruckner through the RSO Berlin. The fortune of my position is that now I am recording with the RSO Berlin. That is, as you know, part of my body constitution, part of my blood. It is an orchestra I had to rebuild after Maazel left; you know, there was a gap of six, six-and-a-half years without a chief conductor. It was a difficult time for that orchestra. I really had to work in an incredible way to rebuild the style of this orchestra. There was great potential there, but a need for an enormous amount of work. And the repertoire! We had to bring back the really main bread-and-butter repertoire of a great symphony orchestra. So this is an orchestra which I am tied to and believe in very much, one I have a special sentimental connection to. And I'm slowly doing all the Bruckner symphonies in concert at the moment.

BADAL: Will you record them at the same time?

CHAILLY: Some of them. There is not yet such an important project tied to this concert series. No! We are just playing. We already recorded the Third, which is coming out in six months. But the RSO Berlin is not only my orchestra, my instrument for the last three-and-a-half or four years, but the orchestra in which I can grow into all the Germanic repertoire: Brahms, Bruckner, Mahler, Beethoven, and Schumann. And you know, we are doing all those cycles slowly over the term of six years. I did a European tour before the recording of the Bruckner Seventh and was given the chance to play it, nonstop, twelve times. The tour was so welcome and so successful from every aspect, and the performance of the Bruckner Seventh was so highly acclaimed that I proposed to Decca that they should think of recording it. They, of course, joined us on the tour and listened to several performances, and they did agree that this was something they would like to put on record. Of course, there was the question how the market would be: would it welcome or be shocked that an Italian conductor was doing Bruckner. I think in the end you have to leave that judgment up to—you have to listen to the record, if you have the courage to spend the money. It is such a bargain.

BADAL: You got it all on one record. Almost every other recording's three sides.

CHAILLY: Although it is the slowest existing on the market.

BADAL: Is it really?

CHAILLY: Yes, I guarantee you. Yes! Look at the timings. There is no one, including Furtwängler, who is slower.

BADAL: That's like Toscanini conducting the slowest *Parsifal* in Bayreuth history.

CHAILLY: Yes, that's so, that's so! When you go to Bayreuth, in the Wagner house, you see the—you know, they write all the timings. I think people should judge the combination of an Italian conductor and a German composer after listening.

BADAL: What do you think you bring to a piece like that that a more traditional German conductor might not?

CHAILLY: My studies on Bruckner started very early, let's say in the last ten years. I went through all the symphonies, all the versions. And I arrived at a state of total madness, and I had to leave it completely for some years. I then started again to look at them, to start conducting them. I think maybe it was a combination between my first studies plus the culture that the Berlin orchestra has in this special period of music. You know, they did Bruckner for so many years with Jochum. Jochum was, and still is a regular guest conductor, and he is one of the greatest Brucknerians who ever appeared. And now Günter Wand is doing the Bruckner Eighth just this weekend in Berlin. So they have just a fantastic tradition in this music. I think they did bring me a lot of culture, a lot of style.

BADAL: So it's a combination of you and the orchestra.

CHAILLY: I would definitely say it's a combination, yes.

BADAL: All musicians should realize that when they are making a record, they are doing something very important because they are making a document that will be available for years. And yet you hear the charge that there are many musicians who don't really realize that. John Culshaw, for example, said that opera singers would show up at recording sessions vocally tired from singing too many live performances.[1] Charles Dutoit says that he doesn't like to record as a guest conductor anymore, that he prefers to record only with the Montreal Symphony. You recorded last weekend with the Cleveland Orchestra, and you are going to record with the orchestra this weekend. Wouldn't you prefer to record with an orchestra that knows you better?

CHAILLY: If Mr. Dutoit wants to record in Montreal, there are may reasons for him to do that, but his example is certainly not comparable to my career. It is very important for me to make that clear. I find it in a way limiting to just have one orchestra to record and perform with when you have a choice of the top world orchestras. Besides the RSO Berlin, other orchestras with whom I record are the Vienna Philharmonic, the Concertgebouw of Amsterdam—whom I am going to start conducting next year in a long series of recordings—and the Cleveland Orchestra. I mean, this is such a superselective level of orchestras, and it gives you such a splendid opportunity. So I won't consider it a risk for a conductor who has the chance and the challenge to have such important orchestras for recording. And I don't think the Cleveland Orchestra knows me that little, because I have been coming over here every year for four years. And there is, more and more, a mutual, easy understanding between us, a fantastic friendship and relationship. The work is very easy, you know, without any special problems or particular friction. This is an orchestra whom I fell in love with since my Blossom debut four years ago, and this love never stopped.

BADAL: Music is an art that exists in time, and if you were to conduct the same piece twice in a row, the second performance would be different from the first.

CHAILLY: If it is immediately after, I don't think so.

BADAL: But a recording will always be the same. Some musicians are bothered by that. Does it bother you?

CHAILLY: Well, the record is a record, of course. You should take the record as an example of a particular way to perform a piece. That's it! I would say, for my part, when I'm convinced of a piece, usually there is a lag of only a few seconds between one concert and another. For example, today the Beethoven Second was exactly the same number of minutes and seconds as yesterday night. This is a question of how you feel. There are great, fantastic conductors who change every night. It's a question of nature; it's a question of opinion. I am one of those who, when I do something, keep the time the same length and the tempos the same. But if I go back to the piece five years later, it might be completely different.

BADAL: How would you feel then about a performance you recorded five years before?

CHAILLY: Well, I really think you should take it as an example of what your performance was in a specific time of your development: youth, age, and so on. But it should not be something forever because it is always nice to see there is a growing and that there is a change of mind. So I don't criticize conductors—and there are plenty of examples—who perform the same piece two times, and it sounds far different, one performance to the other. I find it even more fascinating.

BADAL: Media theorists say that people tend to accept the level of technology they are born into but regard successive developments as a threat. Do you see any danger from the increased application of technology to music?

CHAILLY: I see only a help. I mean, to help the popularity of music. We are never happy with how popular a piece is, an opera is, a singer is, an artist is. And we have this challenge today, this fantastic challenge, to use this technology to make music, classical music, more and more popular. I think the only thing to think about, to dream about, is to one day make *L'Histoire du soldat* or *Andrea Chénier* as popular as pop music. So I really think and believe that this technology today can help music to be more and more popular

BADAL: In his book *The Composer's Advocate,* Erich Leinsdorf talks about a man who listens to a lot of records, goes to a live concert, and doesn't like it because it doesn't sound like his stereo.

CHAILLY: Well, that's a bit extreme, don't you think so? No, I see another danger from technology: the effect it has on the way people compose. That is what makes me very afraid. Why do I say that? Because I'm always interested in avant-garde music; I'm very interested in the avant-garde. And the more I see, the more I go through scores of avant-garde music—I'm not talking of only modern avant-garde Italian music but all the music I'm able to look at—the more I see the effect of technology on composing avant-garde music, experimental music, electronic music. That makes me much more frightened than the fact, if I have to concern myself with an aspect of music, that technology can help bring more and more people to classical music. I'm more afraid of the effect of technology on the composing aspect than on the performing aspect.

Note

1. *Putting the Record Straight* (New York: Viking, 1981), 151–52.

PIERRE BOULEZ

ॐ

PIERRE BOULEZ'S DISCOGRAPHY is a fascinating combination of the predictable and the provocative. As a conductor, he possesses a reputation as a leading force in the performance of contemporary music, and during the 1960s and 1970s—first as principal guest conductor of the Cleveland Orchestra, then as music director of the New York Philharmonic—he challenged and threatened his audiences with a full range of modern fare including music of the Second Viennese School. In a more conservative vein, he also established himself as a superlative interpreter of Stravinsky, Bartók, Debussy, and Ravel. During this period, he recorded primarily for Columbia, and among the expected readings of the Stravinsky ballets and Berg's *Wozzeck* came total surprises (Mahler's complete *Das Klagende Lied*) and major oddities (Wagner's *Love Feast of the Apostles*).

Shortly after the death of Hans Knappertsbusch in 1965, Wieland Wagner invited Boulez to take over his famous production of *Parsifal* at Bayreuth. The chasm separating Knappertsbusch's massive approach from Boulez's leaner, more athletic traversal was immense, and the Deutsche Grammophon recording, drawn from the 1970 season, sharply divided critical opinion. Wolfgang Wagner set the stage for an even more explosive controversy when he engaged Boulez to conduct and subsequently record (for Philips) Patrice Chéreau's provocative centennial production of *The Ring* in 1976. The Boulez-Chéreau partnership also ultimately yielded Deutsche Grammophon's acclaimed recording of Berg's *Lulu*—based on the 1979 Paris production and incorporating act 3 as completed by composer Friedrich Cerha.

Our interview took place in November 1986. After an absence of several seasons, Boulez had returned to Cleveland to perform and record—this time for Deutsche Grammophon—major scores by Stravinsky and Debussy. ॐ

Pierre Boulez conducts the Cleveland Orchestra. Photo by Peter Hastings.

BADAL: Maestro, we all accept that we live in an age dominated by various forms of media. These media have differing impacts on various aspects of our lives. From your perspective, what impact do recordings have on our musical life?

BOULEZ: Well, I suppose there are different ways of answering that. So the first thing is that people who are not in big cities can listen to very good performances. You know, somebody in a small town in Germany or a small town in England or anywhere can, for instance, listen to the Berlin Philharmonic at its best. So that's already something. Second, the repertoire is enlarged. The repertoire of recording companies, even if they are not enlarging it all the time, is broader than the repertoire brought generally to concert life. They record not only composers who are very well known, for instance, but pieces which are not as often performed as others. Also the music of the past.

BADAL: Had it not been for you, we would not know what the third act of *Lulu* sounds like.

BOULEZ: Exactly! Also, I mean old music. Recordings give an opportunity to listen to it. Otherwise, we would never have the opportunity to hear it unless you read music. Then you could get a score and imagine what it should be like. And the third impact recordings have—but that's a negative one—is that they give the idea, especially for people who are not familiar with the score or are not too familiar with the score, that an interpretation is the score. You know, if you hear, let's say, the Mozart Symphony No. 30 in a recording, and you don't have any other recording—well, you think that all the ritardandos that you hear or the accents that you hear *are* the Mozart ritardandos, *are* the Mozart accents. But these are the ritardandos and the accents of one performer, and maybe it is not the symphony, not the symphony by Mozart you hear, but the symphony of Mozart through the performer.

BADAL: You faced the same problem a number of years ago when you made the recording of *Parsifal* at Bayreuth. The only recordings that existed then were two conducted by Hans Knappertsbusch; and to many people, Wagner's opera and Knappertsbusch's performance were the same thing.

BOULEZ: Yes, exactly! Because people thought that Knappertsbusch was *the* truth for Wagner because he was somebody of the old school.

BADAL: He had been Richter's assistant at Bayreuth.

BOULEZ: Yes, exactly. He was supposed to really have the tradition. In my opinion, there are two things about tradition. First, I don't think tradition is transmittable that easily. I mean, what you transmit generally are the exterior gestures, but not very often the inside of the score. Second, I think that our point of view of the score changes according to the generations. A certain generation wants to hear a score done a certain way, and a performer will come who will bring that to their ears. Look, for instance, if you listen to the Bach suites by Casals—you know, who was the first to record them more than fifty years ago, sixty years ago—if you compare those now, you know, to the suites by Bach played in the Baroque style—

BADAL: As we understand the Baroque style today.

BOULEZ: As we understand it, you are perfectly right, as we understand it today—there is a gigantic difference. The notes are the same, but the sound is not the same; the accentuation is not the same; the speed is not the same. And I think good music is able, you know, to face all these different performances. Especially now when we are in a kind of historical obsession. People are obsessed by the idea that we must find the right way to perform music of the past. That's very difficult to find for good reasons. First, people think they are being objective in their interpretation of old music; but they are not. They discover some old book on performance, and they take it like a bible, you know. Well, that's a bible for a short time.

BADAL: When I talked to Christopher Hogwood, he said he blushes to remember that ten years ago he thought the recordings he made were statements forever. He said they were nothing more than an indication of what we understood then about the performance of the music.

BOULEZ: Exactly! And what is to understand? To understand means to approach music according to what you read on the performance of that time. And you try to reconstitute, but that's always a reconstitution.

BADAL: I remember when you conducted *The Rite of Spring* out at Blossom. I still own the recording that you made soon after, but it occurs to me that that is you twenty years ago. I know nothing of your development, as it relates to that piece, since then.[1]

BOULEZ: Yes, of course. A recording, you know, is a picture. You take a picture of a work at a certain time, and ten years later, fifteen years later, the picture will be sightly different. It may not be completely different.

BADAL: If you perform the same piece twice in a row, the second performance will be different.

BOULEZ: Well, yes, certainly. The second performance is never exactly the same, but they are very close. But twenty years later, the piece can really be rethought, and you can have a different point of view—on certain places, especially. Certainly I myself take a recording for what it is: a document which is of the time, for the time. After a while, you cannot consider a recording as a kind of replacement for the score. The score *is* the score, is really *the* thing, and a recording is just a picture of the score taken by somebody.

BADAL: Like John Barrymore playing Hamlet as opposed to Richard Burton.

BOULEZ: Yes, exactly, exactly! In the theater, you have exactly the same problem. If you look at old films, for instance, or pictures of theater performances—let's say you are looking at pictures of Romans. You have your so-called Roman of 1900, then you have the Romans of 1920, the Romans of 1940 and so on. They are not the same Romans. The same elements are there, but you feel 1900, 1920, 1940. Definitely!

BADAL: A recording allows you to take the musical happenings of a moment, freeze them, and repeat them an infinite number of times. Do you think this fact has had any impact on the way musicians make music or on the way people perceive music?

BOULEZ: On the people who perform music, certainly. I think before recordings we were less eager to hear no defect whatsoever. And now if you have a recording and there is a wrong note, or a singer uses too much vibrato or makes a kind of wrong sound, especially when it is repeated and you hear always the same mistake at the same moment. . . . In a concert, you accept the mistake because you very well know that—

BADAL: It's gone.

BOULEZ: It's gone. And if you come to a second concert, maybe there will be other mistakes, but not exactly the same mistakes at the same moment and in the same way. For myself, you know, I am more careful when I make recordings. The attacks, absolutely together! Because you are thinking, more or less consciously, you are thinking, "If I am not perfect for a recording, people will not accept it." And you are more demanding on yourself and on the players than you were before the era of recordings.

BADAL: One also finds that certain kinds of performances repeat very well while others don't. The example I always use is live tapes of Furtwängler. The first time you hear one, you may be swept away, but the qualities which make it so exciting the first time often do not repeat very well. Performances which are not so individual may stand up better to repeated hearings.

BOULEZ: Yes, because they are more standard, let's say. They are less disturbing from this point of view. You cannot be disturbing the same way all the time. When I do a recording myself, I try to do long takes. Of course, you can be obsessed with precision, but if you limit precision only to small beats, you don't—you miss completely an important part of the music. And I think in the old recordings there may be mistakes, but there is always the long line. Nowadays, especially in intricate works, sometimes you feel the tempo is unsteady. You don't hear the cut because the technicians are good enough, but you feel suddenly a drop of tempo which is completely arbitrary and irrational, which has no reason to exist at this point. And you know very well at this point there was suddenly another take inserted which is not exactly in the same tempo as before. You know, there is excitement in the hall because you have an audience, and the participation of the audience makes that performance more exciting, more lively. But for a recording, you have to keep in mind this excitement, and at the same time, you want perfection. That's not easy to have both, the excitement and control all the time. And therefore, for me doing recordings is really a very hard thing. Especially when you repeat things when something was not good, and you have to repeat two times, three times, four times. You know, the passion evaporates. Let's put it this way. If you pay attention to the mistakes and try to be absolutely perfect, the music can lose its impact.

BADAL: Pop and rock music developed styles which take advantage of the recording medium. In classical music, we still record works which were conceived for the concert hall or the opera house. When I talked to Christoph von Dohnányi, for example, he said he felt it was a mistake to perform standard operas on television. He felt we should compose operas specifically for television. Do you think we should be creating serious works which are designed for a given medium?

BOULEZ: It is difficult for me to think in those terms. If you want to take into consideration the technical means, you could be obsolete after a while because the technical processes are in continuous evolution. There is a very typical example from Stravinsky, who was a very practical man. He was commissioned to write a sonata—serenata or sonata, I don't remember. I think it was a sonata for piano. It was to be recorded. And there were not long-play records at this time; there were only 78s. And all the four movements are within three minutes or three-and-a-half minutes. Now that's ridiculous because, especially with the CD, three minutes, four minutes, thirty minutes are nothing. If you rely on technical limitations—that's like someone saying, for instance, "Don't go higher on the piano than C—you know, the third octave—because after that our machine can't take it." So you will write a piece between three and four octaves instead of seven, for instance. And what will be the result? Thirty years later, fifty years later it has absolutely no meaning anymore. Therefore, I think if you are geared too much to the technical aspects of things, you run the risk of having your work outdated by the progression of technical devices.

As far as television is concerned, it is certainly not the best medium to give concerts or operas. Operas more than concerts because in the theater you can do something, you can have close-ups, you know, and things like that. With concerts you cannot do very much, and broadcasts of concerts are generally miserable from an optical point of view. You have a screen with these hundred people—or sometimes when choral works are involved maybe three hundred people—and you hear a big noise but see people like ants. That's really disturbing to me. They also want to have movement because they think, you know, after two minutes, if the camera is absolutely still, it would be boring. It would be boring; but it is not very much more interesting if you see, you know, a close-up of the first violin, a close-up of the viola. And especially with a pianist playing, they make close-ups on the hands. That's terribly disturbing to see only the hands on the screen. While listening to the music, you don't want to look at fingers.

BADAL: Yet a cellist I know was fascinated when I showed her a film of Piatigorsky playing. She enjoyed the close-ups of his hands.

BOULEZ: Oh, that's different! As a document, that's different. If you are going to make a document of a soloist, then you can focus on the bow, on the technique, on the fingering, and on everything else. I would like to see, for instance, a concert—everything on the conductor. For half an hour I could observe the conductor completely. But you have the conductor for thirty seconds, then you have an oboe for twenty seconds, and then you have the hands of the harpist—especially the harp. They like the harp, generally. It is stupid! There are a lot of things which are not really good for television; I agree with that. I think what they try to do very purposefully is to create some activity or some kind of pseudoactivity. It is the worst kind of distraction for me.

BADAL: You said something in an interview a number of years ago, and I imagine it has come back to haunt you: you said that all the opera houses in the world should be blown up. And yet you went to Bayreuth.

BOULEZ: I gave this interview in Bayreuth.

BADAL: The reason I mention it is that several significant recordings came out of your association with Bayreuth. If you felt that way about opera houses, why did you go?

BOULEZ: Because Bayreuth is not an opera house in the normal sense of the word. You know, in Bayreuth you go for the season; you have good working conditions; you are playing only one repertoire; you rehearse and play everything in succession. In most opera houses, you have what they call "the repertoire." And one day they play *Don Giovanni;* the next day they will play *Fidelio;* the third day they will play *Rosenkavalier;* the fourth day they will play *Tosca;* the fifth day . . . and so on and so forth. Never rehearsed! I mean, it's never rehearsed. You have new singers who have never sung in the production. That's a mess, a constant mess. I'm not speaking of the premiere; I'm speaking of the everyday life of an opera house. And if you go, even in the best opera houses, you hear performances of the worst quality. The quality that people accept in an opera house would be unacceptable in a concert hall. If a concert performance would be on the level of an opera performance, people would scream. As for me, it's impossible; this system is impossible. As a matter of fact, I'm not the first one to say this. Wagner himself said it exactly 130 years ago. He wrote about the system of opera houses in 1850 when he was in Zurich.

BADAL: There are those who would say that, as far as that repertoire is concerned, you're not exactly to the manor born. What do you bring to this repertoire that a more "traditional" conductor might not?

BOULEZ: Well, I think I'm more careful, if I may say so, with the texture of the opera and with the relation to the drama. I want the singers to have a lot of expression in a kind of very valid way, and they are not to shout all the time against this big orchestra.

BADAL: Which is not as big a problem at Bayreuth as it is elsewhere.

BOULEZ: No, that's not as big a problem; but it is a problem. You have 120 musicians, you know, and they can make a lot of noise even in the Bayreuth pit. I was especially criticized the first two years. "The orchestra is no more what it was. The orchestra is too soft." Progressively, finally, there was a kid of cohesion between the stage and the pit. It was really drama, and not only an orchestra playing its guts out with singers somewhere on top of it. You know the monologue of Wotan, for instance, in the second act of *Die Walküre!* You cannot always have this brass playing like mad; this poor Wotan cannot shout that type of confession.

BADAL: Also, if we can't understand what he is saying, then we miss information we need so the rest of the opera makes sense.

BOULEZ: Absolutely! He must be able to project the words without any trouble. This also gives a shape to the score. For me, I am very sensitive to texture. You cannot always have this kind of thickness. I'm very much in favor of different types of texture, and I think Wagner is very, very clear and careful with the texture. The number of times he writes "soft" in the score! And even so, when *The Ring* was first performed in 1876, he wrote to the musicians: "You must know the voices are important." So in his time already, there were certainly exaggerations in the volume of the orchestra. And so I think if I take care of the volume, the modification and modulation of the volume, then the singers can also modulate the volume of their voices and the expressions.

BADAL: I think many people know how you came to conduct *The Ring* at Bayreuth. How did the TV production and the recording for Philips come about?

BOULEZ: Well, at first it made a lot of noise. This performance was, I mean, a very disturbing performance of the century, let's say. Chéreau and myself, we really worked five years in a row, and we were always there from the very beginning to the end. And I had a very good assistant, Jeffrey Tate, who makes a career himself now. Especially with a new production, with everything new, you cannot make a good, a completely good performance in the first year. After that, I mean, the more we did it, the more we improved. But the third year, it was already a good performance, and people got interested to have this performance. People began to show their interest in the third year very strongly, and then between the third year and the fourth year, Wolfgang Wagner arranged everything with Unitel, which is based in Munich. After that, it was proposed to do the recording at the same time, to record simultaneously for television and—

BADAL: Then the recording is the soundtrack for the TV production?

BOULEZ: Not exactly. It was taken at the same time, yes, but for television you could not edit in the same way that you could edit for the recording. So the editing of the recording is not exactly the same, because sometimes for the television, they had to take a less good musically take because it looked better—the television aspect was important. For the recording, we could take whatever we wanted. As a matter of fact, the engineer, the sound engineer for the recording was from New York: Andrew Kazdin.

BADAL: He used to do a lot of work here in Cleveland.

BOULEZ: Yes, exactly. They asked me, you know, whom I wanted, and I liked him very much from my New York days, and then he came to do the recording.

BADAL: When a composer records his own works, is that a special document, or is he no different than any other interpreter?

BOULEZ: It's a document. It's a good document, I would say, if the recording is good; but it's not *the* document. First, you know, the conditions for recording are not always the best in the world. Sometimes you are under time pressure, or sometimes you have not really the instrumentalist you want to have. Sometimes you are, you know, cornered in a situation where you cannot get exactly what you want. And of course, you cannot write on the sleeve note, you cannot say, "Well, you know, I have not the best musicians in the world," or "I've not the best conditions, and I've not enough rehearsal," and so on. You have this recording, and that's it. You have to accept that as an object, as a document. Myself, I'm critical of some recordings I've done before because of the lack of time, or sometimes lack of rehearsal, sometimes some weak element in the combination of the instrumental group. That's very possible; all these things are possible.

I remember, for instance, having heard the *Pierrot Lunaire* of Schoenberg which was issued on Philips, I remember—reissued on Philips. The recording was done, I suppose, in 1940 or 1941 in New York. The instrumental style, for me, is very good; but the style of the woman who is telling *Pierrot Lunaire,* the Sprechstimme, is absolutely unbearable because she has always this glissando. And I find that's unbearable. I was told, "Oh, maybe it was related to the style of acting in Vienna in 1910." Well, who cares now about the Vienna style of acting in 1910? Maybe this way of speaking the text was okay for Schoenberg, but it's not okay for me. I still like these documents. Myself, you know, as a composer, when I performed my works thirty years ago, I was not as clear with them as I am now, and I perform them certainly much better now then thirty years ago. That is true; there is an evolution. There are musical gestures which become natural, more natural than before. And I suppose it has always been this way. I mean, when something is new, that's like a jacket or something. You need to wear it for a while, and you get accustomed to it.

BADAL: One of the reasons I bring the whole matter up is that Leonard Bernstein recently recorded his *West Side Story* using opera singers. A number of the reviews were rather harsh, saying that the operatic approach is wrong; and even if the approach is right, these are the wrong singers. What these reviews seemed to be saying, in a way, was that Bernstein's work belonged to the public and the critics but no longer to him. He wrote the work. Can't he perform it how he wants to?

BOULEZ: You know, I don't know this recording by Bernstein, but I can understand the reaction, because operatic singers are—have generally a heavy style of presenting things. They are singing generally things which are heavier, and the volume is also different. The conception of the voice is different. So, if they perform idiomatically, I cannot say. Only Bernstein can say that. But I see also in this kind of trying to get opera singers for something light an attempt to make the genre more noble. I have done the same thing in reverse exactly. Sometimes I've tried to do *Pierrot Lunaire* with cabaret singers, and it came to the most disastrous results because it is—*Pierrot Lunaire* is a cabaret piece, that's true, but it's a cabaret piece which no cabaret singer would ever be able to sing because the musical capacity is simply not the same.

BADAL: What impressed me about some of these reviews, though, was that they seemed to be saying that Bernstein, the composer, misunderstood the nature of his own work, that he was wrong.

BOULEZ: No, no, no, no! You can't say that. You cannot say that he is wrong; you say simply that you find it inadequate. Like you would find, for instance, in a performance of a work by myself. If there is a singer whose style you do not appreciate, you can say, "Well, for me, the style of the voice is inadequate for the work I'm listening to." That's not a question of wrong and right; that's a question of being adequate to the style or not adequate to the style.

BADAL: Accepting or not accepting the recordings of the composer is a game we all play, and we seem to play it somewhat selectively. Speaking for myself, some of the most uninteresting performances of Richard Strauss I have ever heard were conducted by Richard Strauss.

BOULEZ: I can't speak for Strauss, who was really a great conductor, but even with his own music . . . He did not really work on his own music all the time like a conductor. He was conducting from time to time, writing his own music—and writing took him much more time, especially in the second part of his life. It took up much more time than conducting. He was not involved constantly with the problems of performance. When you see, for instance, composers like Bartók and Stravinsky! Bartók was a very good pianist, but I suppose he never devoted so much of his time to his Second Piano Concerto, let's say, as a pianist today. And there are poetic difficulties and pianistic difficulties. But I suppose, you know, he was just studying it for his own performances and then not bothering with it the rest of the time. It was not part of his repertoire all the time.

BADAL: I saw Schuyler Chapin on William Buckley's show, of all places, talking about the recordings of Stravinsky. He said how wonderful it was that we had them because now we knew how he wanted his music to go. I remember thinking, when Stravinsky wrote *The Firebird* in 1910, did he really mean for it to sound the way he conducted it fifty years later?

BOULEZ: No, certainly not. In 1910, he could not imagine himself in this position. It is good we have these recordings of Stravinsky, that's true, but as I say, they're documents. That's all! I have seen him conduct. I knew him, and I have seen him conduct. He was not a professional conductor. He was more a composer than a conductor. So why should we rely on recordings which convey certainly a certain spirit but which convey also a number of defects? And the older he got, of course, the weaker his personality came through because the physical strength was not any more there. And, you know, that's the difference between Stravinsky and Monteux. I have seen Monteux conduct when he was very old, and I have seen Stravinsky conduct when he was very old. Monteux could compensate for his physical weakness because he had a technique which allowed him almost not to move but still control everything, and Stravinsky had not this technique. So when he was younger, you know, the physical strength came through in spite of the clumsiness, I would say. But when the physical strength was not any more there, there remained only the clumsiness.

BADAL: But even taking that into consideration, I felt that Stravinsky was conducting *The Firebird* in the light of everything he had composed since. Your recording is very lush and romantic in a way that his isn't.

BOULEZ: I suppose I can understand how he would take a work of his youth which was influenced by Rimsky-Korsakov, by Scriabin, especially—he wanted to bring it closer to him, and that I am not obliged to do. And therefore, if I take this same course, I never do the reorchestrations of 1945 or 1947—1945 for *The Firebird,* 1947 for *Petrushka*—because I find these reorchestrations are a disaster. But I suppose, you know, with these big orchestras for *The Firebird* and *Petrushka* . . . Dance companies will not have big orchestras like that. The pit was too small, or there was not enough money. So they will make their own arrangements. And I suppose, you know, that it could be very annoying to Stravinsky to hear arrangements made by Mr. X, or Mr. Y, or Mr. Z, and he preferred to have his own arrangements for reduced orchestra. I agree on this point. I can understand the sheer economic necessity for a dance company to have a score which is reduced; but if you are in a concert or in a big ballet company and you have the money, do the original!

BADAL: Media theorists say that people tend to accept the level of technology they are born into but regard further developments as a threat. Do you see a danger to music from the increased application of technology?

BOULEZ: No, on the contrary! I see a benefit. I will give you an example. In the nineteenth century, you know, people were reading scores and playing scores, and there was a direct contact with the music. We don't have that anymore now. People don't play the piano so much. I was born in a very small town, and when I was very young, there were people doing four-hand versions of symphonies by Beethoven or by Schubert. The performances were very poor. You could read the music, but you still had no idea what it was like in performance. And now, through recordings, you get a better idea of what a work is.

It can be compared to reproduction in the visual arts. In the nineteenth century, you had just very poor black-and-white photographs or etchings, but now you can reproduce quite well and quite faithfully a big painting. Even if you don't go to the museum because the museum is very far from your home, you know very well what this painting is and represents. And that's the same for music. I don't know about the future, what will be the improvements or the new discoveries, but I think if you really—if your ideas are strong enough, if your personality is strong enough, you will always be, not a slave to these discoveries, but you will master them, and they will serve you. And that, from my point of view, is what we should have.

Note

1. The recording referred to was made by Columbia. Boulez has since recorded a digital version, again with the Cleveland Orchestra, for Deutsche Grammophon.

ANDREW DAVIS

⸱ᔓ⸱

THE FIRST MAJOR release on Columbia under Andrew Davis's baton was a two-LP set of the three Borodin symphonies coupled with the usual orchestral excerpts from the composer's *Prince Igor*. For a young, still relatively unknown British conductor recording for a major label, it was a shrewd choice of repertoire: relatively familiar music, somewhat removed from the center of the so-called standard repertoire, certainly not overexposed on disc. Davis discussed the early phase of his recording career rather extensively in our interview, making it clear that much of his Columbia discography was selected with similar care.

Though his subsequent move to EMI yielded such significant issues as the live recording of Tippett's *The Mask of Time,* his recent affiliation with Teldec further illustrates how important to a successful recording career finding and exploiting the proper niche can be. The German company promptly teamed Davis with the BBC Symphony Orchestra and, under the heading "The British Line" prominently displayed on the CD booklet, began recording music of English composers—a generally praised series that so far includes works by Vaughan Williams, Elgar, Britten, Delius, and Holst.

Arranging an interview during the Blossom summer season is always a tricky affair, and the fact that Davis was temporarily beyond the reach of a telephone in the Canadian wilderness further complicated plans for this conversation. We ultimately talked on a late August afternoon in 1987 by the pool of his hotel. In spite of the heavy rehearsal load and the brutal heat, he appeared relaxed and casual. His patience and humor received a major test that weekend when a sudden violent thunderstorm interrupted his performance of the Brahms Symphony No. 4 and rendered WCLV's broadcast tape useless. During the intermission, while the elements continued to rage, one orchestra member offered the delighted audience a surprise rendition of "Stormy Weather." ᔓ

Andrew Davis. Photo by Clive Barda. Courtesy of Shaw Concerts, Inc.

BADAL: Maestro, I think everyone accepts the fact that recordings have a great deal of artistic importance. It would probably come as a surprise to people outside the music business, however, that they also have tremendous economic and public relations value for an orchestra as well. Before you went to Toronto, the orchestra really hadn't done that much recording.

DAVIS: No, the Toronto Symphony before I went there had not—apart from some records for the CBC. We still continue to make records for the CBC, and they have a series now called the SM 5000 series. We've made quite a few recordings for them which are theoretically available in stores. I mean, theoretically they have international distribution; in fact, they don't. The CBC has never quite gotten its act together as far as distributing its commercial recordings is concerned. So the orchestra made quite a few of those, although not that many otherwise. Seiji Ozawa recorded a couple of things, I think, with the Toronto Symphony for RCA. He recorded Messiaen's *Turangalîla* and Takemitsu's *November Steps*.

BADAL: He performed *November Steps* here in Cleveland at about the same time.

DAVIS: Oh, I'm sure, yes. I mean, he did that piece all over the place at one time with two Japanese instrumentalists. He recorded the *Symphonie fantastique* also, but that was about it.

BADAL: I'd be interested in the politics of the situation. Did you bring the contract with you to Toronto?

DAVIS: Yes. I had at that time an exclusive contract with CBS. It was an exclusive contract, but it was only for—oh, it was never for more than two records a year. But it was a contract. And so therefore, when I went to Toronto, CBS decided they'd like to make some records there. During the whole time I was under contract to CBS, I was making records both in London and Toronto.

BADAL: It would seem to be a very difficult situation for a young conductor to make recordings. You have to make them to be well known, but you have to be well known to make them.

DAVIS: Yes, that's right.

BADAL: It seems to me that young conductors tend to record on what I call the fringes of the repertoire; there are certain things they will leave alone. The first recordings of yours that I was aware of were the Borodin symphonies. I remember thinking what a good idea that was, because your name was beginning to be known, and that was repertoire that no one else had done at that time.

DAVIS: Yes. All two-and-a-half symphonies, one should say, really.

BADAL: How was the repertoire you recorded in Toronto selected?

DAVIS: Well, you know, I had discussions with CBS at some length about it. As you say, the problem is to find repertoire. I mean, obviously no record company is going to invite some younger man like myself to record Beethoven symphonies and Brahms symphonies.

BADAL: Would you even want to at this point?

DAVIS: Well, no. No! In fact, I certainly wouldn't—although I have recorded three Brahms symphonies in Toronto with the CBC, and I'm quite happy with them. But for a major label . . . Well, I don't think any major label, as I say, would ask for them; and for me, it wouldn't have been right. So then we talked about various areas of the repertoire which were of interest to me. The Borodin symphonies idea, I must say, came from CBS. At that time Paul Myers was the A&R [Artists and Repertoire] guy in CBS. He's actually responsible for signing me up. He had the LSO [London Symphony Orchestra] booked, and someone canceled. So he said, "Okay! We'll get Andrew to do some stuff." So I did. My first record for them was the *Young Person's Guide to the Orchestra* and the Prokofiev *Cinderella* with the LSO. So he and I discussed the Borodin idea, and it kind of appealed to me. I mean, I don't think the Borodin symphonies are great, great, great music, but they are fascinating.

BADAL: And they should be recorded.

DAVIS: Yes, absolutely! They are important.

BADAL: And they should be done well.

DAVIS: They should be well done; and at that time, I don't think there was a complete recording of them. The Second Symphony, of course: there were probably eight recordings of it in the catalogue, actually. That piece seems to have been done quite a lot. But the others—and I think the First has some wonderful things. Beautiful slow movement in the First Symphony. So I was very happy to do them. I think the second record we recorded in Toronto was Janáček: a suite from *The Cunning Little Vixen* and *Taras Bulba,* which is a record I'm very fond of. It never did very well.

BADAL: You've got to be Czech.

DAVIS: You've got to be Czech or . . . not so much that, but that coupling wasn't that successful, I think. Neither of those pieces is really that popular. I mean, you've really got to do the *Sinfonietta* to make an impact. But I'm really very fond of the recording. And then we did the complete *Nutcracker,* which was more popular.

BADAL: You raise an interesting point with the Janáček record. There are some composers, such as Beethoven and Brahms, which everyone records. There are those areas of the repertoire, however, in which we try to match the nationality of the conductor with the composer. We want to hear

Italians do Rossini and Frenchmen do Ravel.

DAVIS: I guess so. Yes, that is certainly true to a certain extent, although I think one can oversimplify. As I say, I'm very happy with that recording; but it never really took off. Then we recorded several other things. The complete *Boutique fantastique* of Rossini-Respighi which, again, is a very, very fine recording, I think.

BADAL: The repertoire of some of your recordings does not seem to be particularly well chosen. I'm thinking of the record with nothing more on it than the Dvořák opus 46 Slavonic Dances.

DAVIS: The one I did with the Philharmonia! Absolutely! And that was never my intention. It only came out last year or two years ago, and it was recorded ages ago.

BADAL: Really?

DAVIS: Ages ago, yes. It must have been at least four years ago I did that, if not five; and they've been sitting on it for some reason. In fact, at one time we were talking about—you see, the problem with the Slavonic Dances is they don't really fit. You can't do both sets on one record.

BADAL: No, you really need three sides.

DAVIS: Three sides. Then you've got to find a filler.

BADAL:. You could probably get them all on one CD.

DAVIS: On CD, of course you could. On a CD you can get seventy-four minutes of music. Anyway, the other major area of the repertoire I recorded with CBS was Dvořák symphonies.

BADAL: Was that ever intended to be a complete set?

DAVIS: Yes! And in fact we recorded them all, and they had cold feet about issuing the first ones, which is too bad because they are of interest, especially the Third. I think the Dvořák Three is really crazy. It has this sort of Tchaikovskian, rather balletic first movement. Very beautiful. Then this wonderful slow movement which reminds one alternately of Berlioz —sort of *Romeo and Juliet* love scene music—and Wagner. I mean, there's a lot of Wagnerian writing: brass and harps and things.

BADAL: I think the last movement of the Fourth Symphony is one of the worst bits of Dvořák I've ever heard.

DAVIS: That's very unfortunate because the first three movements—

BADAL: The third movement is wonderful.

DAVIS: Yes, absolutely. The slow movement and the scherzo. And the first movement is nice, too, but the finale is very weak.

BADAL: When did you record these?

DAVIS: Oh, again, we probably finished them about five years ago.

BADAL: And you can't do anything to get them released?

DAVIS: No, I never had the kind of contract that guaranteed—in fact, after I'd been with CBS quite a long time, when the contract came up for renewal, I said no because it wasn't a particularly fruitful thing for me in the sense of being tied to one company for one or two records a year. It didn't seem to make sense to me.

BADAL: Now you're recording for EMI.

DAVIS: We recorded *The Planets* for EMI last year, and we've just recorded the *Messiah* for them in Toronto.

BADAL: Really?

DAVIS: Oh, yes. This is going to be—it should be out in September or October, I think. Very shortly!

BADAL: Which edition did you use?

DAVIS: Well, when they approached me about recording the *Messiah,* from the word go, I didn't want to do another small one, because there have been several extremely good recordings to come out in the last couple of years with, you know, people like John Eliot Gardiner with his choir and the English Baroque Soloists. I think that's whom he did it with. And Hogwood has done it. And so I thought, no! It's time for us to do a slightly old-fashioned, maybe unfashionable, sort of large-scale kind of *Messiah*. And then, of course, we came to think, "Well, maybe it's time for another Beecham *Messiah*."

BADAL: When I talked to Christopher Hogwood, he said it would be interesting to see a revival of the Beecham-Goosens *Messiah* or the version by Sir Michael Costa.

DAVIS: Yes, well, in fact, I listened to the old recording of Beecham, and really it's "over the top," as they say. I mean, all this percussion!

BADAL: Cymbal crashes!

DAVIS: Cymbal crashes, and there's even a whip in "Thou Shalt Break Them." And string pizzicato all over the place. It's a fabulous piece of orchestration in its own right, but I found it too much. And I looked at Mozart. Mozart is interesting.

BADAL: It's been recorded.

DAVIS: It has also been recorded, and I don't like all of it. I mean, there are some absolutely magic things in it. "The People who Walked in Darkness" is wonderful. The chromatic bassoon, clarinet, and flute writing that he added is absolutely the work of a genius, but some of the other things he did I never liked that much. So in fact, what we did was just use the standard edition in most of the solos, although for the bigger numbers, I used a full string section. I mean, a full symphony orchestra string section—eight double basses and sixteen first violins. And I did that for things like "He was Despised" and "Thou Shalt Break Them."

BADAL: How big was the chorus? Is this going to be one of those big Victorian performances?

DAVIS: The chorus is not quite on the scale of some of the Victorian things, but the Toronto Mendelssohn Choir is about 180 voices, so it's a big sound. And for the really big choruses—about five or six of them, I suppose; certainly the "Hallelujah" chorus and the "Amen" chorus and some of the others—I actually used the Ebenezer Prout edition. There are a couple of clarinets in there, but you wouldn't know. You can't hear them. We actually didn't record in Roy Thomson Hall in Toronto. We did three performances there, and then we moved out to Kitchener, which is where we recorded *The Planets* last year. Neither I nor EMI were very thrilled by the sound of our concert hall in Toronto, so we recorded this out in Kitchener. That meant we couldn't use the grand organ in Roy Thomson Hall, so I dubbed that myself afterwards. It was rather fun, I must say. The boring thing about that was that we had to do it before we edited it, so I had to put the organ parts on all the takes before the editing process could be done. I think it's going to be very exciting. I spent a lot of time editing it, too. I've never actually spent that much time—I've never been so closely involved with the balancing, mixing, and editing of anything as I have been with this, and to me it's really, really fascinating. So I'm very excited. It's a very good cast. It's Kathy Battle, Florence Quivar—

BADAL: You can't do any better than that.

DAVIS: No! So Kathy, Florence—Florence is wonderful—John Aler—

BADAL: I don't know him.

DAVIS: Very good in this kind of repertoire. And Sam Ramey! I'm doing *Figaro* with him in Chicago in a couple of months' time.

BADAL: Which raises an interesting point: You've done a lot of opera work in your career, but very little on record. Is that your choice?

DAVIS: Well, I wouldn't say I've done a lot of opera. I started conducting opera at Glyndebourne in 1973, and I was there every year from 1973 to 1980. I was there again in 1985–86, and I'm going to be there for the next few years, four years, anyway, from next year. Otherwise, I've been to the Met twice, Covent Garden twice, the Paris Opera once—and that was once too many! And that's it.

BADAL: Your opinion of the Paris Opera is shared by some of your colleagues, I guess.

DAVIS: Oh my God! It was the worst experience of my life without question. Anyway, that's another story. So I haven't actually done an enormous amount. I've done a lot of Strauss, and I seem to have been pigeonholed as a Strauss conductor, which doesn't bother me at all actually. I adore that music.

BADAL: You did that little bit from *Die Liebe der Danae.*

DAVIS: Yes, the symphonic fragment, that's right. On the record with Eva Marton—which I quite like, I must say. That was a fun record to make. That was made from three live performances. Which is another thing! For a while a couple of years ago, several people seemed to be very hot on the idea of recording from live performances.

BADAL: Leonard Bernstein still is. I once read of a critic who thought you were more impressive in live performances than you were on record.

DAVIS: I think that's true. I don't enjoy listening to most of my recordings because I think they—and I'm not talking about the most recent ones. I think probably in the last three or four years, I've at least begun to feel more comfortable in the studio. And I don't know what it is. Well, I mean, I do know what it is to a certain extent. One of the things I find—and I'm sure other people felt the same thing; I mean, George Szell hated recordings—

BADAL: I think most conductors from the older generation did, and for very understandable reasons.

DAVIS: Well, I don't know why it should be any more understandable for them than it is for us.

BADAL: On very old recordings, the sound was bad.

DAVIS: Yes, that's true. It's not the sound that bothers me.

BADAL: And in the days of 78s, of course, you could only record things in four-minute bits.

DAVIS: Oh, yes. Sure, sure, of course. That was appalling. But George Szell was never really comfortable after many years of recording, and I think it was probably for the same reason that I dislike it. You know, it's very hard to recreate the sense of performance, especially in regard to structure, if one is always stopping and starting. The overall shape of the piece can very easily become lost. Or one becomes very careful. You want to make sure that something is clean and precise, so you just sort of take a little edge out. And that is something I've really had to fight against, so I think that comment was absolutely right. There are some of my early recordings that I like very much. As I told you, the Janáček one I really enjoy. But that, interestingly enough, was recorded in a very short amount of time, so there's a sense of urgency about it. It's funny. I haven't thought about this a lot lately. I had the feeling for many years . . . My career started very quickly, you know. I first started conducting sort of full time as a professional activity in 1970.

BADAL: That's when you did the Janáček mass.

DAVIS: That's right, *The Glagolitic Mass.*

BADAL: You also had a recording that you referred to.

DAVIS: Yes, and as a matter of fact, it was Karel Ancerl's. I had to learn the piece in two days, so I wasn't above listening to a recording of a performance to help me. That's a piece I've always been very, very, very fond of.

BADAL: It's a tremendous piece.

DAVIS: It's great. A great work!

BADAL: Kurt Masur did it out at Blossom. It was wonderful to hear it outside.

DAVIS: How did the organ sound?

BADAL: Not very good! It was loud.

DAVIS: Yes, that's the only problem with doing it outdoors. I agree with you in every other way; it's tremendous because that's what it's all supposed to be. So everything started very quickly for me, and in a sense I sort of couldn't believe it. There was a part of me that thought my success was sort of indecent. And I think there was a certain insecurity. You know, am I really this good? Do I deserve to be where I am? For some reason that insecurity was particularly apparent in the recording studio and made working there harder for me. I think at this point in my life I've come to terms with it. I've been conducting for some seventeen years, and I think I'm where I am because I deserve to be where I am.

BADAL: Did you have to come up with your own philosophy about working in the recording studio? Do you, for example, prefer long takes?

DAVIS: It depends on what I'm doing. I'm just trying to think . . . Lately, you see, I haven't actually recorded anything like a symphony which has really long, extended movements, not in the last two or three years. We did *The Planets,* of course, which is a major piece, but it's seven shortish movements. Even the *Messiah* is that way, although the continuity of the *Messiah* is very important to me.

BADAL: It must have been very difficult to record it because I'm sure you did it out of order.

DAVIS: We recorded it out of order, but we had just done three live performances. That really makes a tremendous difference, so the shape and structure of the piece and the dramatic tensions are there somehow. It's interesting. It's the first time I've ever conducted the *Messiah,* too. But in a way that was good, because I came to it very, very fresh. There are some pieces which are good to approach that way. On the other hand, there are some other pieces I would not dream of taking into the studio if I had, not only done them several times, but done them several times within the period I was having to work on them. That's another danger, I think, for a young conductor. A company comes to you and says, "We want you to record Dvořák symphonies," for instance, which is what they did with me. A lot of them I really hadn't done very much at all. I scheduled the Sixth and Fifth symphonies several times before I recorded them. Actually, those two, I think, came off almost the best of my Dvořák cycle.

BADAL: I think when anybody makes a recording, I don't care how long you've been a performing musician, you can't escape that sense that it is never going to change, unlike a live performance in which a mistake is going to be forgotten.

DAVIS: Yes, and in that sense the recording is sort of artificial. It's against what music and the performing arts generally are because they seek to recreate something in an instant. It's the same if you go to see a play. It's something that exists in a specific period of time, and then it's gone. Then you've got to do it all over again.

BADAL: Unlike the cinema, for example, which is also always the same.

DAVIS: That's right! And nobody is going to make another version of *Amadeus*. But I'm not questioning the validity of recordings, of course; I think they're great. But there is a certain nervousness that comes with the knowledge that the recording never changes.

BADAL: Listening to a recording in the privacy of your home is a very different kind of experience from listening to a performance in a concert hall. Have recordings changed the way people perceive music or the way musicians make music?

DAVIS: I think there has been a much greater—I mean, accuracy has become sort of the number one consideration almost. Which has been good in some ways, because it has cleaned a lot of orchestras up, so to speak. There are so many great recordings that you could put on. So the orchestral player, never mind the conductor, but the orchestral player, will know that the recordings are there, will listen to them himself, and have a greater sense of responsibility to clean up his own act—collectively, as it were. So I think recordings have done a lot in that regard. But the opposite side of the coin is perhaps this sort of caution.

BADAL: It's a caution that extends beyond execution into the style of the performance itself. One can look back at someone like Furtwängler—

DAVIS: That's right. Fine. Now you get into the question of accepted traditions of performing things, and somehow there has been less deviation than there used to be. It's partly a question of taste and style, you know. Some of the old Furtwängler recordings, for instance, are marvelous; but there's certain repertoire you listen to him do and not only disagree but find totally untenable from a stylistic point of view. So I should say, the refinement of taste is a positive aspect of recordings. Somehow, sometimes you want to get away from that and say the hell with it! Let's hear some really way out bending of phrases and some very strong statement that one can react to either with ecstasy or dismay.

BADAL: Stokowski!

DAVIS: Stokowski, sure. Stokowski is a very good example. I've become rather fascinated with him lately, not really having known a great deal about him. I've just read a very long biography of him.

BADAL: Oliver Daniel's book. Yes, I've read it too.

DAVIS: It opens up, for me, a whole new way of looking at things. The spontaneity of his early career is tremendous. It's totally unrelated to recordings, but he could say, "Fine! In three weeks' time I'm going to program this or that piece." It's a thing of the past. I mean, one can do that under extraordinary circumstances, but I sort of know what I'm doing for the next two years. So there's a certain spontaneity that has gone out of the music business as a result of . . . well, of all kinds of things. Just the fact that there is so much demand for music now, and we're all booked so far ahead. It has become a very commercial industry.

BADAL: How do you feel about historical recordings? Is there anything to be learned from them?

DAVIS: When you say historical, you mean old recordings where the sound is crabby? Sure, because you hear great conductors making great music.

BADAL: Do you have any particular favorites?

DAVIS: Well, sure. I've never been a great collector of recordings either old or new. I don't listen to records a lot. But some of the old Furtwängler recordings I think are fascinating. The Wagner *Ring* cycle he did with the RAI Orchestra in Italy, you know, is to me absolutely mind-boggling. Some of the old Bruno Walter recordings I think are marvelous, especially in the Mahler repertoire. And some of his Mozart I think is fantastic.

BADAL: There are some conductors who come across on records better than others. A friend of mine never particularly cared for Karajan until she saw him conduct *An Alpine Symphony* on PBS. She was tremendously impressed by the visible intensity of concentration. Now, that is a purely visual quality; you don't get it on records.

DAVIS: Yes, and I think that's true. Now, whether Karajan differs in the recording studio, I don't know. I'd be fascinated to go to a recording session of his. In his recordings he always seems to go for a tremendous sort of depth and smoothness. I've heard performances of his that . . .

had much more excitement than his recordings. I mean, I've heard the same piece live and on record. I think he's a wonderful recording artist. Great! I mean, he is great. Just great, great, great! The man is a bloody genius. He's one of the greatest musicians who ever lived. I used to hate his music making, incidentally. I found it so over—I don't know, there was something about . . . sort of a slickness about it. But I think his music making has become more moving, to me anyway, in the last ten years. I think his knowledge of his . . . his realization of his own mortality—I don't know. Anyway, you know, it's presumptuous for me to talk about Karajan, I think—for any of us to talk about Karajan except in the most adulatory terms. The man is incredible, and I find him now an absolute miracle.

BADAL: Could we talk about *The Mask of Time*? Now that's a live recording.

DAVIS: That was a live recording, and it was not intended to be. And a piece like that, in a sense, I would have—

BADAL: I would think a piece like that would have been a tremendous risk in a live situation.

DAVIS: It was a tremendous risk, and I wasn't at all happy about it. I actually stuck my neck out and said to the recording company and to Michael—and I love Michael Tippett, I think he's a very, very great man, and we're good friends—but I said to him, "I want to be able to say when I hear the tapes—I mean, I want power of veto." We had planned to record it in the studio. We were going to have so many days' rehearsal, and then we had a couple days in the studio to record it.

BADAL: What happened? Was it an economic decision?

DAVIS: It was an economic decision. They couldn't raise the money, which I found absolutely maddening. And then at the last minute, after the recording sessions actually had been canceled—just for union purposes one has to release dates if they're not definite—when it was too late to salvage those recordings days in the studio, they came up with enough money to do this compromise, recording it live. As it happens, it turned out very well. There are some things in the performance that are less than 100 percent spic-and-span, but the spirit that comes across is phenomenal. It is wonderfully exciting, and I must say the EMI engineers did a great job. I haven't actually listened to the whole thing since it has come out. I've got a CD at home, and I've listened to most of it. But I haven't had time to hear the whole thing. It's wild! And very moving. I think it's a very moving piece, the second part especially.

BADAL: Did you worry about the acoustics of the hall?

DAVIS: Well, no. I mean, I know the Festival Hall very well, and the EMI people all know it well enough. That wasn't the concern to me. The sound is certainly good enough, and it has a certain amount of clarity about it which is very good for a piece like that. It's not the most sensuous sound, perhaps, but that can be tampered with a little bit. But there is a sort of richness in some of the climactic moments that I think is very impressive.

BADAL: Did you conduct the premiere?

DAVIS: I conducted the European premiere. It was commissioned by the Boston Symphony and Colin Davis, Sir Colin conducted the first performances in Boston. Actually, at that time there was even the possibility of those tapes being used for a recording which, again, I gather didn't happen for financial reasons. Then I did the European premiere in the Proms, and then this, the second performance, was the one which was recorded—the same forces, but in the Festival Hall. I just did it in January in Toronto, incidentally.

BADAL: How did it go over?

DAVIS: It went over very well. Michael came. Oh, the usual number of people left the hall. You know, ten movements, and after each one some people said, "That's enough for me"; but that's what you'd expect in North America. Well, anywhere with a subscription! They didn't leave in huge numbers, and the response of everyone who didn't leave was overwhelming. Overwhelming! Because what the piece sets out to say, and says, in my view, tremendously successfully, is very profound. I mean, it is the only piece I know this century that really sets out so overtly to talk about the great issues: where man came from and where he is going, what he's doing, what he has done, what he has achieved in both positive and negative ways, and what that tells us about the light and dark sides of our natures.

BADAL: How do you feel about recent developments in recording technology? Some people still argue about the suitability of the digital process.

DAVIS: I like it. I like the sound it produces. Again, its main success has been in terms of clarity, I think. The thing one tends to lose—and, actually, people have found ways around it—is a sort of depth. It's a kind of voluptuousness that comes somehow from the richness of the lower register, and when digital recordings first came in, what bothered me was that everything seemed to be very toppy. You know, very high. Great presence of all the upper frequencies.

BADAL: Painful almost.

DAVIS: Yes, painful! And bearing no relationship to what one hears in any concert hall. This is the philosophical question you were asking earlier, I think. Have recordings affected the way we think about making music?

And I think they have, in the certain sense that we all have now got in our ears certain sounds that you only hear on a recording. That gives one a slightly artificial view of what an orchestra does sound like. So then, you know, people actually try to reproduce that in a concert hall, which has made some orchestras, I think, a little too bright. They've lost that wonderful kind of . . . what's the word I'm looking for?

BADAL: Depth! The Vienna Philharmonic at its best.

DAVIS: Yes, this sort of depth. The Vienna Philharmonic, that's right. And that's the kind of orchestral sound I would rather listen to than any other.

BADAL: Media theorists say that people tend to accept the level of technology they are born into but tend to regard further developments as a threat. Do you see any danger from the increased application of technology to music?

DAVIS: No I don't. I mean, we do know that there is the serious potential threat to the livelihood of orchestral musicians in the sense that computers are now able to reproduce, to a certain extent, the sound of an orchestra, and they're getting more and more sophisticated all the time. I think this is a threat in terms of making music for television shows.

BADAL: The music for some TV shows and some films is obviously electronic.

DAVIS: Yes, that's right. But this is never going to threaten a symphony orchestra in terms of performing and recording the great spectrum of classical music. Of course, people have been experimenting. Morton Subotnick is an interesting composer, for instance, who has made some interesting experiments with incorporating—

BADAL: Should composers write serious music for the recording medium like rock artists do?

DAVIS: No, I don't believe that. Well, that is to say, it may well be that a composer will come up with a concept that is not realizable except on record. In that case, I would have to say he has got to do it. I mean, if this is his vision, and it can only be achieved in that medium, then it's got to be that way. It's unfortunate, I think, that this would then be an experience denied somebody in a concert hall. But I don't think recordings will ever be any kind of serious threat to the world of concert giving. That question was first asked so many years ago, and I think it has been so convincingly proven that, if anything, records have had an advantageous effect because they have made more people fascinated by the world of orchestral music. And as your friend said, there's no substitute for seeing Karajan conduct *An Alpine Symphony.*

ERICH KUNZEL

⌁

ERICH KUNZEL'S REPUTATION received an enormous boost in the late 1970s when he and the Cincinnati Pops began recording for Telarc. The Cleveland-based company established its early reputation with a sonically spectacular series of digitally recorded blockbusters, and Kunzel blasted his way into public awareness and onto the *Billboard* charts with Telarc's recording of Tchaikovsky's *1812* Overture. His subsequent repertoire for the company has embraced a wide range of imaginative projects, including collections of light concert pieces, American musicals, and special assemblages of music from television shows and films such as *Round-Up* and *Chiller.* Today, along with Arthur Fiedler and John Williams, he is one of the most popular and widely known "pops" conductors.

Our conversation occurred in June of 1988 at Severance Hall during one of Kunzel's regular visits to the Blossom Music Center. Before his arrival, he had maintained a schedule that would have exhausted an itinerant vaudeville performer: eight concerts in as many days, according to Severance Hall's public relations staff. His grueling workload had obviously left him unaffected, for he sailed through the interview on a veritable tidal wave of energy and enthusiasm. After the interview, he took the short jaunt out to Telarc's Beachwood offices and signed an exclusive ten-year contract. ⌁

BADAL: Maestro, I'm sure most listeners know you through the rather spectacular series of Telarc recordings you have made. How did that association come about?

KUNZEL: Well, Bob Woods was a student in Cincinnati, and he had seen a lot of my work there. The time came when he and Jack started the company, and he came to us.[1] At that time, we were recording for Moss Music Group—Vox Records.

Eugene List and Erich Kunzel record Gershwin's *Rhapsody in Blue* for Telarc in January 1981. Photo by Sandy Underwood. Courtesy of Telarc International Corporation.

BADAL: You still do, don't you?

KUNZEL: No! Oh, no.

BADAL: I guess I'm thinking of Pro Arte.

KUNZEL: But that was Rochester, not Cincinnati. In any case, when the company started, we recorded the *1812*. They came down and recorded the *1812* and *Capriccio Italien*. And that was, of course, a phenomenal success.

BADAL: It still is.

KUNZEL: Oh, yes.

BADAL: Especially now on CD.

KUNZEL: And actually at the time, in the early 1980s, all the classical record companies were just about to fold. I mean RCA Victor, the whole bunch. It was the *1812* that saved Telarc, because without that record, they would have gone ka-flukey too. In any case, then Bob realized the commercial value of the Cincinnati Pops Orchestra. Fiedler was gone, John Williams—those records with the Boston Pops were not selling that phenomenally, and there was room in the market for the Kunzel-Cincinnati collaboration. That's how it all began.

BADAL: Over the years, a definite Cincinnati Pops profile seems to have developed. Something like *Round-Up,* for example. This wonderful bunch of numbers from movies and old TV shows grouped around a Western theme and set off with spectacular sound effects. Did this profile just sort of happen, or was it planned?

KUNZEL: Actually, it just happened. I can give you a for instance. Bob and I plan, more or less, for four years. We throw some things in and delete sometimes; but right now, in September, we're going to record—I think the album actually will be called *Victory at Sea.* We're doing five sections of *Victory of Sea,* and the rest will be essentially a compilation of various things about World War II. And Bob more or less left it to me to decide what else should be on the album. Well, we put in *Casablanca* of Max Steiner because the film took place, you know, during the African campaign. We'll do the *Warsaw Concerto* because that was used in *Suicide Squadron.* Actually, in a couple of movies. So, I've got some movie things. I've got *Valiant Years.* That was the documentary of the life of Winston Churchill that Richard Rodgers wrote music for. So rather than just doing a suite from the *Valiant Years,* I went and got Winston Churchill's actual speeches that he made over the CBC. We're cleaning them up. So rather than just playing a suite from *Valiant Years,* you're going to hear his voice. Then I thought, "Well, listen! What started the whole damn thing?" Pearl Harbor! The bombing there! And then that famous speech of Roosevelt's, that "Day of Infamy." So I went and got his speech. And so you're going to actually hear these important speeches that were given at the time all this happened. Then I thought, "Well, we've got to have *The Longest Day.*" And then the march from *The Bridge on the River Kwai.* We're going to have that. So I'm actually going to have a whole ROTC unit come in and march. We're going to have marching! It's just like *Round-Up.* You get a feeling of character, of what it was like. It was a war! It was tough! We're going to have sixteen-inch guns booming in the thing too. So you'll get marching, whistling, guns, speeches—not just music, music, music.[2]

BADAL: This is certainly not a typical pops album.

KUNZEL: It's the Telarc–Kunzel–Cincinnati Pops way of doing things.

BADAL: I understand it was largely at your suggestion that Katharine Hepburn was engaged for the *Lincoln Portrait.*

KUNZEL: Well, at first we both wanted Gregory Peck. Gregory Peck had a very bad incident doing it in Los Angeles. I don't know what happened, but he said no. Well actually, the first choice was Ronald Reagan. We asked, and they said no because of the commercial business. Then I went to Gregory Peck, and then we were at a loss really. And then Bob came up with James Earl Jones. Very notable! I said, "Wait a minute! We have twenty commercial recordings with men doing it. I want a woman to do it. Lincoln is not here anyway." And then I said, "Well, who has won more Academy Awards than any actor or actress in the world? Katharine Hepburn!" So I went and called her up, and it took me two years to get her to say yes. But it worked, and it's amazing.

BADAL: I'm sure you know that the recording got some bad press because of the quality of her voice, and I must admit I was put off at first. I think, however, that a stock method of delivering the text has evolved over the years, and she rethought it entirely.

KUNZEL: She got words out of that which I've never heard before. The press was mixed. Well, I mean, some papers like the *Washington Post* and the *San Francisco Chronicle* said it was one of the finest renditions ever. People were just used to men, to male voices. I think that was the problem there. They didn't—the people who didn't listen to her interpretation, they just listened to her voice—which was wrong! The reason for choosing her was her mastery of the English language. You know, she's so intelligent, especially with words. Actually, you know, having another actor do it, like James Earl Jones, probably that record would have gotten sort of lost among the twenty other *Lincoln Portrait*s that are now out. But I think because Katharine Hepburn—

BADAL: It did get noticed.

KUNZEL: Absolutely!

BADAL: I take it from everything you've said that you are involved in the selection of all the sound effects on your records.

KUNZEL: Bob and I do it together. We both come up with the nutty things. I mean, he doesn't know about this marching stuff; I'm going to tell him all this today. On the other hand, a lot of things in *Round-Up* he came up with, and I didn't know about them. We both contribute beautifully. I mean, in that sense it's a fantastic marriage, the two of us. We know we have to have perfection. That's our basic principle. We even switched the opening around in *The Sound of Music*. It makes it a better opening too. We open now with just nature sounds and then "The Hills are Alive." Then we go to the abbey scene, and then this thing called "Nature Music" which was never used in the Broadway show. I found it in the Library of Congress. Eight bars that had never been played! This is the first time it has ever been recorded, the first time it has ever been played.

BADAL: I was going to talk about *The Sound of Music* later, but since you bring it up, we'll talk about it now. Leonard Bernstein really started something when he recorded *West Side Story* with a cast of opera singers.

KUNZEL: There's a difference here. I wanted to do *The Sound of Music* because my wife is from Tyrol where it all takes place, and I've been there so often. But the score of *The Sound of Music* is a little bit more operatic, so once we settled on it, the problem of casting came around. Well, the only person—I said, "If I can't have Von Stade, I don't want to do *The Sound of Music*." Because it is a mezzo role, and it has got to be light. And what sold me on Von Stade was, you can buy the Metropolitan Opera version of *Hänsel and Gretel* on tape, and I saw Von Stade doing Hänsel. You know, bouncing around. Youthful! And that magnificent voice she has! When I saw that, I said, "That's Maria." And, of course, it turned out she's just fabulous.

BADAL: Given her age, didn't you take something of a risk with Eileen Farrell?

KUNZEL: No, no, not at all. I know Eileen very well. She was my first choice, but she said no. And that broke my heart. She said, "I'm not singing anymore." Well, a lot happened. She went into the hospital; her husband went into the hospital while she was there. And then he died. She had to go back in for an operation. It was a year of just chaos. I called after that year. Her final concert was with me two years ago in Cincinnati; and I called after all this turmoil had happened and said, "I want you to be the Mother Superior." And she said, "No! I'm never going to sing again." That broke my heart, it really did. I called her about six months later; it was just a fluke. I said, "Let me try Eileen again." And she said, "Yes, I'll do it." And that's how we got Eileen.

BADAL: I heard "Climb Ev'ry Mountain," and the hint of age in the voice is very moving.

KUNZEL: Yes, there are a few things about that. First of all, you have to remember that the Mother Superior—in the role, in the story—has to be a lady who has been around a long time. She's running this whole abbey. So it's not a youthful—it should not be a youthful sound. It should be one of stature. Secondly, when we look at all these crossover record-ings, the one person who started it all was Eileen Farrell. *I've Got a Right to Sing the Blues!* She told Rudolf Bing to go to hell, and she did the first one. So it seemed very appropriate that she be on this album. And the others, I wanted a European type of thing. You know, someone with a German accent for Von Trapp. And Hakegard is so dashing, and he did a beautiful job. His "Edelweiss" is so charming. And then Barbara Daniels as the bitch, so-called; you know, the countess. I know Barbara because she was my student at the conservatory in Cincinnati. Now, of course, she's a great star at the Metropolitan Opera. She has a bitchy sound. That's why I chose Barbara. Every person had to be meaningfully cast; each person was cast with real perfection in mind.

BADAL: There are a number of people who would maintain that opera sing-ers should not be singing American musicals.

KUNZEL: But when you say opera stars singing musicals . . . an opera star and a Broadway musical star can be one and the same person. It's just a human voice. And of course, there have been crossovers: you know, Helen Traubel, Ezio Pinza, and quite a few others. It's just a matter of how you use the voice. Very quickly, during the first rehearsal, Von Stade came in too big on her first number. I said, "No! Lighten up completely! I don't want your voice to travel more than three feet away from you. It's not supposed to fill—" Music Hall is very big; it seats 3,800. I said, "You're going to have a microphone right here, at least for the performances. That same style that you're going to use in the performances, you're going to use on the record. There's not going to be one iota of difference in production." And she adapted immediately! She's so intelligent. So opera stars can be musical stars if they're intelligent. Some singers aren't intelligent, but I had a great cast.

BADAL: I gather that establishing a "correct" text or score was very impor-tant to you. Musicals are not often treated with that kind of respect. You said you even found music in the Library of Congress?

KUNZEL: This is the complete *Sound of Music.* There are two versions: the original Broadway version and the Hollywood version. So in the Holly-wood version there are three additions. Hammerstein didn't write the new words; Rodgers wrote the words and music. There's the song that Maria sings, "I've Got Confidence in Me." So I added that. And then there's the duet that they sing, "Something Good." So those two. Plus the big organ beginning of the wedding procession that Rodgers wrote for Hollywood. These three things I added to the Broadway show. Now, what came out of the Library of Congress . . . The original scores in the Library of Congress are not under Richard Rodgers, but under Robert Russell Bennett.[3] We got a Xerox copy of the original, so actually I conducted from the Xerox of the originals. And we found—I always wondered about this. Here you have the opening abbey scene, and then from there you are supposed to go up in the Alps with Maria dancing around singing, "The hills are alive with the sound of music." Well, there had to be some sort of nature thing to get there. And I said to Bob, "All right! What I want to do is this. After we finish the 'Alleluia', let's just have the sounds of brooks and birds. Then we'll go to 'The Hills are Alive.'" When I got the score, I found Richard Rodgers had written eight or ten bars, I can't remember, of—right at the top, it says "Nature Music." It was there! Right there! And it's very flutey and this type of stuff. We still added the birds as color, but the exact piece I wanted to bridge that gap was there. And it's wonderful! The other thing they left out of both the versions, there is a song, a duet, "An Ordinary Couple." But there's a sixteen-bar intro to that which was never, ever done on Broadway or in Hollywood. And it's, "If ever we are married, I'll love you" and things like that. Von Trapp says this to Maria, and it's beautiful. They're such meaningful words. This is before they get married. He actually says, "I'll be your everything," and then they talk about an ordinary couple. But that introduction is so important to the plot. And so again, you know, it was never performed, but I put this in; it's on the record.

BADAL: Are you ever bothered by the people who call the sound effects on your records gimmicks?

KUNZEL: Well, just look at our catalogue. There's a lot of stuff. I know everybody thinks, "Well, here we've got *Grand Canyon,* and we have thunder. We've got *Straussfest,* and we've got all the popping champagne corks and everything else like that." And of course, we don't even have to mention our *Star Wars* type of things. The sound effects—whatever we do—above all, have to be in good taste. If it's not perfect, we just won't do it. It has to be . . . it has to belong. It's got to be there for a reason. It makes the whole record a jewel. Now, if people call that a gimmick or whatever, fine! Let them call it what they want. To us, it's a part of the whole picture, and it's an important part.

BADAL: And your records have been very successful. Many of them have been on the *Billboard* charts.

KUNZEL: We have seventeen releases now; fifteen have been on the *Bill-board* charts. Now that's a damn good record. Fifteen of the seventeen have been on the Billboard charts. Do you know which two haven't?

BADAL: I . . . well, no!

KUNZEL: *The Battle Symphony!* Even though it has consistently sold very well. It just goes right along. It's a money maker; they all are. And *The Stokowski Sound.*

BADAL: Really!

KUNZEL: And this is a very interesting phenomenon. I don't mind if you print this because it's an actual true fact. I used to do recordings with the Rochester Pops on Pro Arte—no longer because I'm exclusive now with Telarc and Cincinnati. But in any case, my first album with Pro Arte was a Christmas album; my second album was a Leroy Anderson album called *Syncopated Clock.* It went to number two on the charts. At that time, there was only one CD chart; now, of course you know, there are two. But at that time, there was just one. It went to number two on the charts. It was number two for about six weeks; but it was more or less on the charts for the whole year. *Syncopated Clock* was on the charts for about forty weeks. That same year, *The Stokowski Sound* came out; it never made the charts. At the end of the year, I got my royalty statements from both companies. *The Stokowski Sound* sold more units than *Syncopated Clock.*

BADAL: That doesn't make sense.

KUNZEL: Doesn't make sense! In other words, it probably didn't have a quick burst of sales; it just generally sold the whole year and sold more than *Syncopated Clock.*

BADAL: I love *The Stokowski Sound.*

KUNZEL: Oh, it's our favorite. I mean, as far as showing off the real sound of the orchestra in the hall. There are no gimmicks in that one; there are no sound effects. It's just the pure Stokowski sound.

BADAL: Are you comfortable working in a recording studio?

KUNZEL: Well, I don't work in a studio; I work in a hall. This is our secret. Well, it's no secret because we tell everybody. The orchestra sits—in the rehearsal, in the concert, in the recording session—in exactly the same place. Everything is marked. Microphones are put in the same place, at the same angle for everything. Nothing gets changed. So in other words, we're not messing around with anything. For example, when we did the overture album. I can't . . . You see, we do concerts before the recording sessions. I can't give my audience eight overtures in a row. So the overtures were planned through various recording sessions over two years. I did an overture here and an overture there, and the sound is like they were done at the same session. The simple reason: everybody is sitting in their same chairs; everything is marked. And that's what makes it so easy. When we do a recording session, for us it's the same as doing a concert.

BADAL: I imagine you have everything down to a system.

KUNZEL: The only thing is, I make a log. And every person on every music stand, everyone in the booth, has a copy of the log. We do such-and-such a piece, let's say, from 10 to 10:15. Then playback! Then we maybe fix something, then go to the next thing. There's an absolute log we follow very strictly; but of course, sometimes I run out of time at the end because I've misjudged something, perhaps, or something like that. But we're very, very systematic. It's very easy the way we do it, and we get a lot done.

BADAL: I assume you believe in long takes.

KUNZEL: Bob lets me do what I want in that sense. For example, I have to be very careful of my brass—not to overuse them. Maybe I'll switch to another piece, a softer string thing. Then I'll go back to the brass.

BADAL: Movie and TV actors often become typecast. Do you ever feel that you have been typecast by your success in the pop repertoire? Do you sometimes want to do a Beethoven symphony?

KUNZEL: I do conduct one sometimes.

BADAL: Would you record one?

KUNZEL: I don't know if I should. No, I don't think I should. We have enough Beethovens. Essentially, if you look at what we've done with our Cincinnati Pops–Telarc catalogue, every release is something different—with the exception of our *Star Tracks* things. We have a *Straussfest;* we have an overture album; we have *Orchestral Spectaculars;* we have *Round-Up;* we have a Hollywood thing; we have *Grand Canyon Suite;* we have *Rhapsody in Blue.* Every release hits at a different market, a different segment of the audience. Our catalogue is so diverse. And it's continuing. Coming out right now is a thing called *American Jubilee,* an Americana album. A Mancini album is coming out. You're going to hear the glorious sound of the hundred musicians, over a hundred musicians, in the Cincinnati Pops Orchestra playing his arrangements. It's going to be fantastic! We're doing the war album; we're doing a chiller album in October. We have so many good things coming. I can't—I shouldn't really say, but everything that we've got coming up is fantastic.

I'm recording a record a month for five months starting in August. August, September, October, November, December. Five months, five albums we're doing in Cincinnati. And that's a lot, because a lot of work and preparation goes into each album. There's an Irving Berlin tune! I can't remember what it's called; it doesn't matter. I have to go to a vault in a Philadelphia warehouse and meet with the trustees of the Robert Russell Bennett estate to get the two-and-a-half-minute piece that I want to record in September. I'm doing this on July 16. I just want that Bennett version, and it's locked up in a vault. I mean, I will go through anything to make a record perfect, and I love doing it. A lot of preparation goes into every record. We just don't go and get the music. Look at all these film things! There are going to be a lot of film things in the chiller album. There's a lot of work to getting film scores. I once sent John Williams into his own filing cabinet to get . . . In our third space album called *Star Tracks II* we wanted to do "The Planet Krypton" from *Superman.* It sounds a little bit like *Also Sprach Zarathustra.* Well, I talked to John, and he said, "We did that in London. Try the London studios." We called London, and they said, "Well, listen! You know, those orchestra parts have long been destroyed, and there is no way we can get that music." I called John again and said, "Listen! Have you by any chance— did you save a duplicate score?" And he said, "I always Xerox everything, but where to find it! Let me work on it." He and his secretary went into his attic in his Hollywood home to a filing cabinet to get "The Planet Krypton." We got it copied, and we recorded it. When we want something, we go after it.

BADAL: Media theorists say that people tend to accept the level of technology they are born into but regard new developments as threats. Do you see any danger to music from the newer technologies?

KUNZEL: No! I think as we progress into the twenty-first century . . . the electronics have become so sophisticated; the world has become so sophisticated in everything from cars to planes to brains. We love electronic gadgets; we love perfection. And we have just about achieved it in recordings. So people are very enthusiastic about the new CD market, and that market is increasing because people are so stupefied at how true, how pure and perfect the sound can be. Recording techniques have gone to astronomical heights of perfection. We're at a zenith, I would say, in the recording industry, and I think things cannot go anywhere but to a higher zenith.

BADAL: But isn't there a danger that sound has become so perfect that people listen to the sound, not the music?

KUNZEL: I think they are one and the same. I mean, I record musically; I don't record sound.

BADAL: But you have no control over how people listen to the recording.

KUNZEL: No, they can listen in the washtub; they can listen in the bathroom; they can listen in the car; they can listen to it any way they want.

BADAL: And as I said, isn't there danger that people are only hearing the sound—especially Telarc's wonderful sound—and are not really hearing the music?

KUNZEL: Well, no! What they are actually hearing when they hear a Kunzel–Cincinnati Pops record is the sound that I get on the podium. Now if they were right there where I am conducting, that's the sound they would hear. That's the kind of sound balancing that we do at Telarc. So actually what they are getting, for the first time, is the pure sound that Erich Kunzel gets on the podium. For the first time in the history of recording, at least in Cincinnati, a person is hearing the orchestra exactly the way the conductor is, not the way some yo-yo in the sound booth is. No longer do we have this technique of putting microphone by oboes, by second violins, by violas and all this sort of garbage. No! We've always had fake sound before; now it's true. There are just three mikes behind me, and I balance the orchestra for me. No one in the world hears exactly what I hear at the time I'm on the podium. No one in the violin section, no one in the trumpet section, no one in the auditorium can hear the orchestra the way I do. And that is what we are capturing in sound, and that's what's great.

Notes

1. Robert Woods and Jack Renner are the co-founders of Cleveland-based Telarc International Corporation.

2. Much of this was eventually left out.

3. Orchestrated *The Sound of Music.*

LEONARD SLATKIN

ᴊᴏ

LEONARD SLATKIN HAS enjoyed a particularly successful career in the studios. Over the years, he has recorded for three major labels, and each of those associations has yielded significant results.

He achieved his first major success recording for Telarc. At a time when the company was still building its reputation largely through sonic spectaculars, Slatkin and the St. Louis Symphony recorded Dvořák, Ravel, and other bits of standard, unspectacular repertoire. Ultimately, he and his forces also tackled the first two Mahler symphonies.

His move to EMI produced a series of recordings devoted to American music: Barber, Bernstein, and Copland—complete recordings, rather than just the suites, of *Rodeo* and *Billy the Kid*.

When our interview took place in August of 1988, his association with RCA was still in its infancy. Considering the moribund state of the label's activities at the time, the alliance has proved remarkably successful. As Slatkin remarks in this conversation, he transferred the American music series begun at EMI to RCA; records of Copland, Ives, and Piston have since followed. The operatic activity to which he alludes finally produced the recent release of Puccini's *La Fanciulla del West*. Though hardly the first to do so, he has even challenged British domination in English music with a complete cycle of Vaughan Williams symphonies and major works by Elgar.

The circumstances under which this interview occurred were hardly conducive to a relaxed, thoughtful exchange of ideas. On a typically humid summer evening before a Blossom concert, Slatkin emerged from the final rehearsal clearly hot, exhausted, and hungry. With barely a couple of hours to spare before the concert, he charged through his dinner and my questions at the same time. ᴊᴏ

Leonard Slatkin *(foreground)* at a recording session of Ravel's *Bolero* for Telarc in April 1980. Photo by Allan Penchansky. Courtesy of Telarc International Corporation.

BADAL: Maestro, when you were studying conducting at Juilliard, did anyone ever tell you that your ability to advance in the profession would at least partially depend on your ability to land a recording contract?

SLATKIN: No! I never thought I would advance in the profession. I really didn't expect that conducting would give me much more than a bit of occasional work. I was planning to couple it with work in composition, perhaps even in the film industry. But fortunately, I had enough experience when I was growing up, watching sessions with my parents in all the different musical media.

BADAL: The business end of recording is becoming so important. Is this something you simply have to live with?

SLATKIN: Of course you have to. If we look at this past season, for instance! Do you really, honestly believe that Mr. Solti desperately wanted to record the *1812* Overture?

BADAL: The performance certainly didn't sound like he was much interested in doing it.

SLATKIN: That's the point. We all do it. And what does he get in return for it, or perhaps, what did he get in the past? *Moses und Aron!* I can cite you examples of pieces I didn't mind recording—as I'm sure he didn't mind or others haven't minded—but that I did in order to be able to accomplish other projects. For instance, there will be forthcoming on RCA a complete *Swan Lake. The Nutcracker* did very well for us. I think *Swan Lake* is a good score, but not in its entirety, at the same level as *The Nutcracker,* for instance, and it was not a very high priority with me to record a complete *Swan Lake.* But it does enable me to record the Shostakovich Eighth in September, which is certainly not going to be a big seller.

BADAL: When a friend of mine heard I was going to interview you, he said, "Ask him how he got RCA to record Elgar's *The Kingdom.*"

SLATKIN: It's very interesting. I had done the piece a couple times here in the States, and when I was asked to do a set of concerts with the London Philharmonic last season, I asked if I could do *The Kingdom.* It was that simple. Originally, we had the Shostakovich Tenth down on the other program, because that's a piece I do a lot, and I wanted to do it. And they said, "No, our concert series that you're on is tied in to something sponsored by the Sunday *London Times.* And what we do is try to record the major symphonic work later on a new label called Virgin Classics"— which has just started in England. And so they said, "Could you suggest something else, perhaps?" I suggested Walton One. Now, at that time, our commitments with RCA were not quite so firm as they seem to be now, and RCA said, "Well, if you really wanted to record Walton One so badly, why didn't you tell us in the first place?" Well, at the time, no one could know that the recording was tied in with the concert series. So RCA said, "In that case, would you be interested in recording *The Kingdom* since we're there anyway?" You have to understand the new head of RCA, or BMG Classics as it is now called, is an Englishman, Michael Emmerson.

BADAL: BMG?

SLATKIN: BMG is the parent company of RCA now. Based out of Munich. And he simply thought it would be an interesting work to have in the catalogue. It hadn't been recorded since Sir Adrian Boult did it, which has, of course, now been reissued. I didn't press to get it done. It's very interesting; this is one of those things. I had the same reaction that everybody else had. "Gee, you really want to record *The Kingdom*?" And they said yes, and I said, "Terrific." They said, "It will be great." The thing could use a new recording, certainly a different approach. Not that Mr. Boult's wasn't wonderful! It's a terrific approach; I just have other ideas coming from a different generation, a different set of musical circumstances. Meanwhile, it spawned a whole Elgar project. I mean, people got really excited about—the performances were received very well by the audiences, the orchestra, and the press. So we've already recorded the *Variations,* a couple of the overtures; the Second Symphony gets done in February; the First Symphony gets done in August next year; and then come *Gerontius, The Apostles,* and all the others.

BADAL: I'm a little surprised that RCA would undertake a project like that at a time when Previn and, I think, a few others are doing Elgar cycles.

SLATKIN: But a lot of the Elgar that I do is stuff they're not doing. In order to compensate . . . you need an *Enigma Variations* to set off the other pieces for those who will be interested to see what I do with those works. I think if we took the attitude that no one should bother to do what someone else has recorded, we'd have nothing left, would we?

BADAL: Did recording play a part in your musical education, either formally or informally?

SLATKIN: Well, both. My parents were heavily involved in the recording industry, so from a very young age, I was on the soundstages at Goldwyn, Warner, and Fox watching the techniques of recording—the preparation process, the recording process, the editing process. I always knew about recording; it was always a part of our lives. My parents virtually made their reputation from recording in their string quartet. So, yes, recording played a very big part.

BADAL: The older generation of conductors was very ambivalent about the whole idea of recording. Younger conductors, however, who have grown up with recordings seem much more comfortable with them: what they are, what they can be.

SLATKIN: Oh, I'm not so certain! I think we maybe know a little bit about what they are, but I think most young conductors have no idea what they should be at all. The majority of recordings I hear tend to be very dry and antiseptic with no sense of trying to recreate the performance. They're a little bit too polished and clean for me. I can't think of any record I've made where there are not one or two little errors that are passed over just because I prefer the sweep of a particular passage. I'm not striving for perfection; I'm trying very hard to produce a record that reflects how I felt about that piece on that given day. And I try to get the best I can out of it.

BADAL: Some conductors say they conduct differently for recordings than they do for concerts.

SLATKIN: You have to. You have to. I perform differently from concert to concert.

BADAL: If you conducted the same piece twice in a row, the second performance would be different.

SLATKIN: Hopefully, it's not going to be the same. Sometimes certain tempi that you can get away with in a concert hall because of the tension and atmosphere that are there don't come off in a recording. I find sometimes what I might do a little bit slower in the concert hall is a little bit quicker on a recording just because I don't have an audience there.

BADAL: Leonard Bernstein has wrestled with a similar problem for years.

SLATKIN: So maybe that's why he opted to do his recordings from concerts, although they usually do come in for a day or two after performances and patch, to cover up audience coughs and little bleeps and little other mistakes that happen. In some cases, it works; in some cases, it doesn't, I suppose.

BADAL: There was a time when the interpretive differences in, say, Beethoven's Fifth were very great. Today, the interpretive range seems much narrower. On the one hand, you could say that this narrowing was simply a natural evolution of our understanding of how the piece should be played. On the other hand, it seems to me that you could say that recordings are establishing interpretive boundaries.

SLATKIN: Well, that's true to a certain degree. Certain conceptions about tempi have changed. As each generation passes, however, certain stabilizing forces come to pass. I think you can almost begin to categorize Toscanini as the turning point when things began to come, to a certain degree, into focus. And now they are out of focus again if you really think about it. For instance, Mahler has now become quite—you can have a discrepancy of up to 15 minutes in a symphony on recordings.

BADAL: There's a three-minute difference between Knappertsbusch and Richard Strauss in the *Fliegende Holländer* Overture.

SLATKIN: Well, Strauss had a different set of problems to deal with, didn't he? He had to get the music down in a certain amount of time. Also, I've never found composers really could be trusted in tempi anyway, especially in their own work. If you look at Stravinsky and hear two recordings of the same work, the tempi change. Usually, a composer, for the most part, is recording a work quite a good deal after it was written, and so the original impulse, the creative juice, has passed. They're looking at it from afar as opposed to the time they created it. Bernstein is a good example. Just look at the timings over the course of, say twenty or thirty years from when he first recorded a work of his until now. You'll see two-, three-minute differences. It's amazing! I think people say "That was too fast" or "That was too slow" in relationship to how they think it should go. But for the most part, I'm finding that conductors these days are tending to look towards extremes. For me, it's either too fast or too slow, moving away from middle ground.

BADAL: You feel this way about recorded performances?

SLATKIN: Oh, yes. Do you think Kleiber's Beethoven sounds like anybody else's?

BADAL: Carlos Kleiber?

SLATKIN: Yes.

BADAL: No, I guess it doesn't.

SLATKIN: Solti's? Look how slow the new Ninth is, for instance.

BADAL: No slower than his older one.

SLATKIN: Oh, yes! The third movement is much slower, much slower. Now we have the penchant for listening to things in so-called authentic performance practices on original instruments. Look at the "authentic" performances now with . . . what's his name?

BADAL: Hogwood?

SLATKIN: Norrington! Now there are fifteen minutes chopped right off the Ninth Symphony. Just like that! Even with the repeats!

BADAL: I've seen films of Toscanini, Furtwängler, Knappertsbusch, Walter, Klemperer, Erich Kleiber, Mengelberg, and Koussevitzky. Whether you agree with their performances or not, they all had one thing in common: They were visually very compelling. Even the ones like Walter and Kleiber, who were certainly not charismatic in the sense that Toscanini was, compel your attention.

SLATKIN: It was a different era.

BADAL: You see conductors today who are not compelling in the same way. They may be superb musicians and have wonderful techniques, but they don't compel your attention. Recordings separated the visual side of a performance from the aural side. Could that account for this difference?

SLATKIN: I don't think so. I think that the conductor used to be a great figure of mystery. And you tell me how many interviews you actually saw in the press with a Knappertsbusch or a Mengelberg. You didn't know much about the conductor other than he was the conductor. Period! Even Toscanini! There are not many interviews. Bruno Walter? Not much! So this hugely mysterious figure would come out on the stage. That quality would transcend into recordings: you know, the mystery of the whole thing. Szell was the same way. There just isn't that much in interview form. And as we come to the close of our century, with so much attention from both the print and aural media, the conductor, as any artist now, is much less a figure of mystery. They are more communicative with their public in a manner aside from the musical one.

BADAL: I'm not sure that deals with the issue.

SLATKIN: All right, let's put it a different way. Look at the conductors now who still create that mystery. Kleiber! How many interviews with him?

BADAL: None.

SLATKIN: Giulini?

BADAL: Some.

SLATKIN: Not much!

BADAL: I think we're talking about two different things. I'm talking about the podium aura.

SLATKIN: Doesn't matter! In that era, the earlier era, that mystery . . . it was a mystery to everybody whether you heard it on a recording or not. You didn't know anything about the artist. You didn't know.

BADAL: I haven't seen Kleiber live, but I've seen him on TV. I find him enormously compelling to watch, but that has nothing to do with what I know about him or don't know about him.

SLATKIN: I wonder.

BADAL: There is simply something about him which is very compelling.

SLATKIN: This is true; he has an unbelievable communicative power. I know what you mean, but that's part of the art of conducting—the ability to transcend, transcend the music in a way. For some, for me, it distracts from the music, unfortunately, but there's—you find yourself drawn into it. Who can say what that is? Who knows? It doesn't matter whether it's recording or live. I know many conductors who don't record well.

BADAL: Some kinds of performances don't repeat well.

SLATKIN: We also have a backlog of more performances out there in the marketplace. For instance, I find now increasingly I'm not listening so much to the older conductors anymore because there have been so many other statements of all this music; but when I was growing up, listening to Toscanini or Bruno Walter, or whoever it was, was a fascinating experience because there wasn't that much else. Just a few conductors out there to listen to. Now, everybody's out there, including myself. There are records I don't want to listen to again.

BADAL: When conductors begin to make records they usually avoid repertoire that has been frequently recorded such as Beethoven and Brahms symphonies.

SLATKIN: Most companies wouldn't want it.

BADAL: When you recorded the Mahler First and Second for Telarc, Mahler was still, to a degree, the property of people who had Mahler reputations. Did that bother you when you recorded them?

SLATKIN: No. Why? What good does it do? I never feel I'm in competition with anybody when I make a record. In general, I make a record because I feel I've arrived at a point where I have something to say about the piece and that it will probably not change too much in concept in the next few years. That's the reason I recorded all the Rachmaninov works when I did; that's the reason I'm doing so much Shostakovich right now and so much Elgar. I'm at a point in my life now where I'm very secure in the music and wish to get it down as I feel it. There are other pieces I don't want to record yet. I would be remiss if I started a Beethoven cycle because I'm not settled in all of them yet. That doesn't mean I don't do them well, but I don't do them to my satisfaction yet. A recording represents a time. Look how many conductors are already . . . Von Karajan has done his third or fourth Beethoven cycle. Solti is around his second Mahler cycle. You know, everybody is rerecording. I'm not so anxious to rerecord things. I've been approached, though, in a certain repertoire. But I just don't think about who else did what, and I certainly don't listen to anyone else's performance before I go into a performance of a work or before I record it. I have memories of certain things, and—

BADAL: Are there any special performances you've heard which come back to haunt you?

SLATKIN: You mean of other conductors? Oh, sure! Earlier in the year, I heard Bernstein do a *Le sacre du printemps* with the Tanglewood Festival Orchestra—not the Boston Symphony, the students. I can't say it came back to haunt me; but since then, whenever I do the piece, I really—I'll never get it that way. I'd love to, but I can't. It was too good. It was just

. . . In a way, I may put the piece aside now for a few years because it was that good. There's no reason to do the piece now. This was, for me, how it should go.

BADAL: We still play games over what kind of conductor we went to record a certain repertoire. We want to hear a Frenchman do Ravel and an Italian do Rossini. You did that cycle of American works for EMI. Now, I'm certain you were happy to do them—

SLATKIN: Oh, I was very happy to do them; it was our idea.

BADAL: But as an American, did you feel a little typecast?

SLATKIN: No, because I have the Russian stuff and the English stuff going. We have Brahms out there; we have all kinds—I think we do a varied repertoire. But when you stop and think about truly outstanding collaborations of conductor and orchestra, you almost inevitably also tie them to a certain repertoire. For instance, Solti–Chicago! Ormandy–Philadelphia!

BADAL: Ansermet and the—

SLATKIN: Suisse Romade. Karajan–Berlin! Even though we do, of course, a broad repertoire, I wanted with my orchestra anyway—If we are going to make a mark in this world, I felt it was important for us to be known for a certain kind of repertoire. If you want to call it typecasting, you can call it that, but I told the orchestra that we won't neglect anything at home, but on the road, this is what we are going to do primarily. And it's exactly what we do, and it serves us very well.

BADAL: Are you comfortable working in a recording studio? Some conductors are very straightforward about certain problems they have to work to overcome in this studio.

SLATKIN: First of all, I don't—unless I'm in Europe, I don't record in a studio; I record in our own hall in St. Louis. So we're all comfortable. We know the acoustics; that's no problem. All the recordings that we make in St. Louis, and now even the ones I do in Europe. A lot of European orchestras are surprised because I take the American technique into the sessions. If it's a symphony, I do one complete take of the whole work without stopping.

BADAL: Simon Rattle does the same thing.

SLATKIN: Then I go back, do another take of a movement, and then fix it up as to whatever needs fixing. So in general, I have a concept of the whole work to build from. Although once in a while, I start and I feel it's just not going right, so I stop and do it over again. I mean, not technically, but somehow it's not happening. I'll just stop, take a little break and come out and do it again. It's the easiest way to work. Once in a while, a certain piece will be easier to record in sections. We did *Appalachian Spring* that way; *Swan Lake,* of course, would have to be done that way. But symphonic works tend to be very long arcs.

BADAL: Does it bother you not to have an audience present when you record?

SLATKIN: No. We rehearse that way anyway, and it's not a problem there. So recording is not much different. And if I don't need an audience at rehearsal . . . I try to keep a certain intensity in rehearsal. It's relaxed, but it's also intense. My orchestra knows that what they get from me at rehearsals is at least what they'll get in performance. Sometimes, they get a little more. But I never just sort of—first of all, I never rehearse sitting in a chair. So I'm always conducting as if it were a performance to start with. But I always give as much as I can, and recording is the same thing. I just do the best I can. We still know that people are in the booth listening, so whether we can see them or not doesn't matter. We know they're there. The recordings that I consider the most successful are the ones where we somehow feel the presence of an audience.

BADAL: Which ones do you consider have that quality?

SLATKIN: Oh, I think the *Thomas Tallis Fantasia* of Vaughan Williams is like that. I think the D Major Brahms Serenade we did is like that. I think Mahler Two is like that, certainly. A couple of the Rachmaninov things have that, too.

BADAL: How did your association with Telarc come about?

SLATKIN: They came and visited us. They approached us many years ago. It was when they were just starting out, and they wanted to take on another ensemble other than the Cleveland Orchestra. I don't quite know why. They just came; and it turned out to be very, very fruitful for everybody for the time it existed. I'm sort of sad not to be able to work with them right now, because I always enjoyed the integrity of the company and what they stood for, but my repertoire has moved in a direction that Telarc just isn't into, anyhow at the moment. But there's always the future. Maybe in the future. But I think we're looking at most of the marbles going into the RCA department anyway—including, possibly, the EMI repertoire. I may shift it over to RCA. When you stop and think about— you wouldn't know anyway because most of this stuff isn't out yet, but I'm doing about nine or ten records a year. Now that's a lot. And of these, five or six are in St. Louis. A year! That's a lot for an American orchestra. And there's my relationship with the London Philharmonic and now the Bayerischen Rundfunks.

BADAL: I didn't realize that.

SLATKIN: Yes, I'm doing a lot of concerts with them and things like that. And so there's a lot of talk about some recording projects in that department, too, including, possibly, operas.

BADAL: That's one of those orchestras that can play beautifully for the right conductor, but can also play very badly.

SLATKIN: I know! We had a good time. First of all, I had the worst cold in the world. I got off the train; it was snowing, and I was sneezing, and my eyes were tearing. And somebody came up after the first rehearsal and said, "You know, this is the first time we ever made a conductor cry from the first rehearsal." It's a very nice kind of relationship. We've had a good time, and I enjoyed it.

BADAL: Media theorists say that people tend to accept the level of technology they are born into but regard subsequent developments as threats. Do you see any danger to music from the application of all these rapidly changing technologies?

SLATKIN: Well, if that were the case, then we'd still be in the mono age we started with when I grew up in the 1950s, without stereo! So I've seen, at least in my own lifetime, I've seen us go through phases. I've seen us go in and out of quadrophonic quickly.

BADAL: Ironically, at least as far as I understand it, digital techniques make quad a much more plausible option.

SLATKIN: They do, they do! Although I still think it's artificial. I mean, it was a gimmick then; it's a gimmick now.

BADAL: How many people had a room big enough for it to work?

SLATKIN: I had a room, but it didn't work. The assumption is—I would not want the Philadelphia Orchestra in my living room; I don't want the so-called reality element. I want the best recorded sound I can get, not the best live sound I can get, in my living room.

BADAL: Well, we all accept this to a certain extent.

SLATKIN: No, we don't.

BADAL: We talk about realistic sound, but we don't really mean it in that sense.

SLATKIN: Well, if we truly wanted realistic sound, we would find great hypocrisy, especially in the early music movement, because the sound you hear on period instruments in a recording is quite another matter from what you would hear in a 2,700-seat concert hall.

BADAL: The sound would be much louder on records.

SLATKIN: It's louder, yes; but it's all a big distortion for me. I find it all—not fraudulent, but I find the acceptance of it a little bit too superficial.

BADAL: Companies also went in for some rather bizarre orchestra seating arrangements when they recorded things in quad.

SLATKIN: Who wants to sit in the middle of the orchestra and listen? And if you sat in the middle of the orchestra, you wouldn't hear everything. But we do make seating adjustments when we record choral works a lot of the time. You'll find the chorus is in the back of you, behind you. So you kind of conduct sideways.

BADAL: Does that bother you?

SLATKIN: No, not if everyone knows it real well. You're trying to get the best recorded sound you can, so you make adaptations when you can. I'm not sure I would want to record the Verdi Requiem in that manner, but who knows? But back to your original question! I'm keenly interested in the changing of technologies. I did grow up with a sound in my ears—not so much a recorded one, but a live one—because of my upbringing. I know the kind of string sound I'm looking for, and I try to find a way to get that in recording. Sometimes I get it; sometimes it doesn't happen.

BADAL: Is that your fault or the fault of the guy in the control room?

SLATKIN: It can be mine. It depends on the day. It can be everything. Humidity sometimes enters into it, how the players are feeling one day. The sound can change, the sound can change. But for the most part, I'm finding the sound I'm getting on discs is pretty close to what I imagine in my head. A lot of people don't like it. They don't think it's quite high tech enough. I don't like so much multimiking because you don't have very much control on the stage. Then there's more control in the booth than there is on the stage. I would rather make my own mistakes out there than have somebody fix them right and left for me.

BADAL: What do you think of this debate that still rages over analog versus digital techniques?

SLATKIN: Oh, nonsense! High-speed analog and digital—I can't tell the difference. I like to think I have relatively good ears, and I can't hear any difference. The only thing I find with digital technology—and this is where the past does come up—is that we're certainly not used to hearing that clean a sound on a record. Without hiss, without distortion. We're just not used to that. Sometimes—it depends on the company, and it depends on how things were done—I find it's a little bit too . . . let me see . . . not high oriented.

BADAL: Of course, that was one of the main criticisms of digital sound.

SLATKIN: Yes. It's not quite the word I was going to use for it. But for me the beauty of digital technique really is not the ability to capture the wide spectrum of sound so much as it is the ability to really get something as soft as you like. Although even there, I found I couldn't do what I wanted. I've done certain things so soft that they said, "No! We can't have that. It's too soft. It won't come out on the disc." And I said, "Even on a CD?" They said, "You can't play something quite that softly." Obviously we still have a ways to go with the technology! DAT [digital audio tape]? Who knows? At the moment, it sounds like another five years before it even takes. I'm not sure how viable it is. The argument seems to be more of a copyright problem than it does a sound technology problem.

BADAL: Are you ever bothered by the thought that people become so wrapped up in the sound that they don't hear the music?

SLATKIN: Oh, yes! I think the problem of people bringing that sound into the concert hall is the biggest danger there is. "It didn't sound like my record" is the worst thing I ever want to hear. A concert experience is an entirely different matter for me. The way an orchestra sounds in a hall with an audience there and with the tension is very different from recording in terms of the sound itself. And let's face it: a recording also unfortunately makes the assumption that everybody's ears are the same, and they're not. Everybody hears things differently.

BADAL: In a way, the assumption also seems to be that all our playback equipment is the same, too.

SLATKIN: True! But all these things come into play. No two people are going to hear a performance in the same way, both emotionally and simply aurally. It's not going to happen; it's not going to happen. I hope it's not, anyway.

NEEME JÄRVI

No ONE COULD have predicted a decade ago that Neeme Järvi—a little-known recent Estonian emmigrant—would eventually become one of the most frequently recorded conductors, producing a discography of such bulk as to rival the outputs of Bernstein and Karajan. Those two eminent maestros, however, recorded for the major companies and built their vast legacies around the core of the standard repertoire; Järvi, in a totally unique fashion, established his reputation by exploring obscure and unusual repertoire (Stenhammar, Tubin, Glazunov) on relatively minor labels (Chandos, BIS, Orfeo). Part of the Järvi method also involves recording entire cycles of compositions, not just isolated works: all eight Glazunov symphonies for Orfeo, the four Berwald symphonies for Deutsche Grammophon, all seven Prokofiev symphonies—including both versions of the Fourth—for Chandos.

As Järvi's fame grew, he not only began making more determined forays into the standard repertoire (Shostakovich, Richard Strauss, Schubert), but found Deutsche Grammophon growing more receptive to some of his less-than-traditional notions about recording projects. Hence the cycles of symphonies by Rimsky-Korsakov, Berwald, and Borodin.

At the time of our interview in July of 1990, his recording plans with the Detroit Symphony were obviously in a state of flux. In this conversation, he raises the issue of to which label he and that ensemble would devote their services, a question ultimately decided in favor of Chandos. He also mentions the possibility of recording American music with his then-new ensemble; and with a typical Järvi flourish, he subsequently picked music by William Grant Still, Amy Beach, and Duke Ellington. ✄

Neeme Järvi. Courtesy of Columbia Artists Management, Inc.

BADAL: Maestro, I saw you conduct here in Cleveland back in 1981. It was a performance of *Samson et Delila* with the Met. Almost no one knew who you were then, but today you are very well known. Part of the reason, of course, is that you have made so many recordings. Did your recording career start in the West?

JÄRVI: Before it was Melodiya only.

BADAL: Really!

JÄRVI: A lot of Melodiya recordings when I was in Estonia. All my previous work was done for Estonian radio, also some Melodiya recordings.

BADAL: What did you record for Melodiya?

JÄRVI: All Estonian music. It was not even known in the Soviet Union, in Moscow, because that was some kind of local policy: if you do Estonian music, let's keep it in Estonia. But Estonia was absolutely a closed country in the Soviet Union, a military place. There was no way to show my art outside. Only in Estonia. I went out sometimes to conduct orchestras abroad. Not, of course, in the Soviet Union, but abroad, certain Eastern Bloc countries. It was not enough for me. Also, I thought we had very interesting composers in Estonia, for example, Arvo Pärt and Edward Tubin and Heino Eller, and all this, until quite recent time, was unknown outside Estonia.

BADAL: You raise an interesting question. A lot of the repertoire you have recorded is hardly mainstream: Tubin and Gade for BIS, Glazunov for Orfeo. How did you and these labels decide on this repertoire?

JÄRVI: When I came to the Western world, it was 1980. Then I got work— of course, not in America because nobody knew me here—but with the Gothenburg Symphony Orchestra. There was a free position, and I started to work there. Immediately, I thought it would be nice to do something interesting there because Gothenburg is not Stockholm; it's not Copenhagen; it's not Oslo. It's the second city of Sweden . . . very good tradition! I was very proud to be conductor of this great orchestra founded by Wilhelm Stenhammar, so we started with Stenhammar. Who was Stenhammar? I didn't know very much about Stenhammar. Only his Second Symphony was known. So we started to make recordings of this composer's music, to show the musical world there is not only the Second Symphony and the Serenade, but also the First Symphony and a lot more music. Also Edward Tubin! An Estonian composer who lived in Sweden. For me, it was some kind of national—I had to start to show music from my country. I started with the Tubin Symphony No. 4. It has an interesting history. The Tubin Symphony No. 4 never existed before the recording. It was burned during wartime. He brought this score to Sweden, but it was so badly damaged, it was impossible to play. And I said to him, "Listen! You have to make that No. 4 ready for me because I want to record all your music."

"Ah, don't play that music," he said. "It's bad music, and it's not necessary to play this. This is rubbish. I have much better things."

But finally he did it for me, and it was first played in Bergen. It was the same time when we recorded the Stenhammar First Symphony. And the same time the BIS recording company picked up the Stenhammar symphony, live recording, they took the Tubin Symphony No. 4 from Bergen and released these two records. BIS will do these things, not because there is money, no, but it is the kind of company which—really enterprising! And the company was successful with these two pieces, so we did the complete symphonies of Stenhammar and Tubin. I thought it was much more interesting to introduce something unknown to the musical world than to start to repeat the same mainstream repertoire. But very soon, I went to the Scottish National Orchestra. And my predecessor was Alexander Gibson, who played a lot of Scandinavian music in Scotland. In concert and recording. Sibelius's music! My way was to start something else in Scotland which was new for the Scottish orchestra. Russian repertoire!

BADAL: The Prokofiev symphonies.

JÄRVI: Prokofiev symphonies for Chandos. We started there first. And now we have done almost fifteen records, about fifteen records; and we are going to celebrate Prokofiev's anniversary in a great way because there is a lot of good music.[1] We have recorded all the symphonies and symphonic poems. And then came Shostakovich, and then a lot of music like Balakirev with the City of Birmingham Orchestra, and then a lot of Glazunov music, and Kallinikov, and slowly we came to Dvořák. Slavic music! Dvořák comes closer to the mainstream, but still not in the mainstream because there are not very many people who have recorded the complete Dvořák symphonies. It is usually Seven, Eight, Nine, and that's it! It is good to be together with a creative record company which understands artists very well. Maybe it needs mainstream repertoire in its catalogue, but it understands an artist who wants to do something really unusual. I give the ideas to them, and they pick up the ideas immediately.

BADAL: Do you feel smaller companies are more receptive to these ideas than larger companies are?

JÄRVI: Yes, of course. As I see it, all these big labels are repeating each other.

BADAL: You did the Berwald symphonies for Deutsche Grammophon.

JÄRVI: Yes, and this is also unusual. But it is—actually I'm very happy about that. Deutsche Grammophon also now picks up my ideas, ideas which are not very mainstream. Now come things like Shostakovich Thirteen, Fourteen, and so on. Things like this. Grieg! Not only *Peer Gynt,* but the Symphony, *In Autumn,* and things like this. Interesting things! A very good relationship with the Gothenburg Symphony Orchestra and Deutsche Grammophon.

BADAL: I've actually heard people say, "It's wonderful that Järvi records all this unusual repertoire, but he does so much recording—standard repertoire *and* unusual things. He just can't know all this music very well when he records it.

JÄRVI: They are not right! Because this recording process started only ten, let's say six or seven years ago. But I have lived a long life before this. I have conducted for thirty years, but my recording started only six years ago or seven years ago.

BADAL: Your Western recording activities.

JÄRVI: My Western recording activities. I did a lot of recording for Melodiya before. I know very well all the classical, mainstream repertoire. I studied at the Leningrad Conservatory. Every day for five years in conducting classes, the talk was of Richard Strauss, Brahms, Beethoven, and all these. Mahler and Bruckner! And when my teachers, Nikolai Rabinovich and Yevgeni Mravinski—these were all our pedagogues—were youngsters, student fellows, Otto Klemperer and Bruno Walter and Knappertsbusch came to Petrograd. These conductors conducted every week, every month in Petrograd.

BADAL: Was this during the 1930s?

JÄRVI: It was the 1930s, yes—1920s, 1930s, the Nazi time. They came to conduct in Soviet Russia; they all came to Russia. Bruno Walter did lots of performances at the Kirov Theater—Maryinsky Theater! Later it was the Kirov. And our repertoire was that classical repertoire. But I'm not very keen to do this repertoire now because everyone is doing it. I think it is much more interesting to introduce to the musical world pieces which are less known.

BADAL: Do you feel it's important to perform a piece in concert before you record it?

JÄRVI: Very important! And I have done almost everything that way. That means I do it first in concert, then record it. Some . . . some pieces I have recorded cold, let's say. Just recorded them! But basically I perform a piece first always. But I perform it—not in Berlin, not in New York, not in famous capitals, but in the smaller places. People don't know about these performances.

BADAL: Let me ask you a philosophical question. When you record Gade, Tubin, or Berwald, those recordings become documents of the music, but when you record Schubert, Brahms, or Richard Strauss, don't those recordings become documents of you as a musician?

JÄRVI: Yes, of course! I try to show myself when I do these Richard Strauss recordings, how different I am from other conductors. I don't like very much to do him like some kind of—some people think there is a tradition, and they ask, "Why is he doing it that way?" I do it my way. "Why is he rushing here? Why is he doing these things here?" Because it's my view. Why not do it that way if it is persuasively done?

BADAL: Your recent recording of the Franz Schmidt Second with the Chicago Symphony on Chandos was a live recording. I'm not exactly sure how many of your recordings were live. How do you feel about live recordings?

JÄRVI: It depends on the situation, which orchestra is playing. Live recording can be very, very good. If you know it's a live recording, you behave like it's a recording studio and not so much like making a concert. I tell you, the Stenhammar First and the Tubin Fourth . . . we didn't know if these performances were recorded or not. I knew the Schmidt was being recorded. We recorded it during the four performances, and we had to put it together some way. I knew we had to be careful. In a live concert, you don't care about—it's natural music making.

BADAL: Furtwängler's live recordings were far freer than his studio recordings.

JÄRVI: And I think he didn't know his concerts were being recorded. You hear seeking, freedom, a free interpretation. Every performance is different. He was a creative person. He was doing things that were all the time different. There were no rules. "This tempo must be this way; that tempo must be this way; it must slow down in this way." No! It is some kind of feeling . . . it comes so naturally. And this is what you feel from these concert tapes of Furtwängler.

BADAL: Do you feel records have an important role to play?

JÄRVI: I think so. I think so. Because we can't play all this repertoire in—if you look at some American orchestras, for example, all these big cities and smaller cities have the same team of soloists, same type of repertoire, same style of repertoire. And the main talk is that audiences want that. Audiences want this or they will not come to the concert. I think it is necessary to make right repertoire policies, to play proper proportions of things in concert, to try to play in concerts unusual works as much as possible. And then try to record them, the unusual pieces. Also, recording is the only way unknown orchestras come to be really known orchestras. You can't travel so much; you can't tour so much. There is a financial situation. You can't go everywhere, but recordings can.

BADAL: What would you like to record with the Detroit Symphony?

JÄRVI: Very difficult, yes—good question. It all depends on the financial situation in Detroit. As you know, a financially troubled orchestra! But I think we get a good level of orchestral playing already, and we get support from society. We need to do recordings, and not . . . maybe go to American music. There are a lot of interesting things in America.

BADAL: Ives?

JÄRVI: Yes, Ives, of course! But he is more known. There's the whole Boston school and a lot of composers which are not—are underrecorded. And we might try to do something like this. Piston and Creston. A lot of interesting things.

BADAL: What label would you record for with the Detroit Symphony? The orchestra used to record for London.

JÄRVI: Yes, I know. But I'm committed until 1993 with Chandos. And we will see how things develop later.

BADAL: Media theorists say that people tend to accept the level of technology they are born into but regard subsequent development as threats. Do you see any danger to music from the application of all these rapidly changing technologies?

JÄRVI: Danger? There is no danger. It is good to have new developments. If there is digital sound now, if there is a compact disc era, or whatever, that's a good thing. I'm a little bit unhappy, though, because I sometimes miss this regular 33 stereo sound, real natural stereo sound. It is a little bit artificial for me sometimes.

BADAL: Digital technology?

JÄRVI: Digital technology. The very first CD . . . when I heard it, it was a very artificial feeling for me. And if things go ahead that way, maybe it's not good.

BADAL: There have always been people who feel digital sound is artificial.

JÄRVI: Yes, artificial. This kind of very close . . . where there is not space enough. Sometimes space is made artificially, and that I don't like. Artificial space! But that you feel immediately is wrong. But maybe that also develops a little bit. For example, more spacious sound. It depends very much on the hall, where you are doing things, where you are recording. A hall like the Concertgebouw. Marvelous, beautiful recording, and with digital equipment. A marvelous sound.

Note

1. The one hundredth anniversary of his birth in 1891.

BIBLIOGRAPHY

Antek, Samuel. *This Was Toscanini.* New York: Vanguard, 1963.

Böhm, Karl. *A Life Remembered: Memoirs.* Translated by John Kehoe. London and New York: Marion Boyars, 1992.

Bruno Walter in Conversation with Arnold Michaelis. Columbia Masterworks, BW 80.

Chapin, Schuyler. *Leonard Bernstein: Notes from a Friend.* New York: Walker, 1992.

Chotzinoff, Samuel. *Toscanini: An Intimate Portrait.* New York: Alfred A. Knopf, 1956.

Culshaw, John. *Putting the Record Straight: The Autobiography of John Culshaw.* New York: Viking, 1981.

————. *Ring Resounding.* New York: Viking, 1967.

Daniel, Oliver. *Stokowski: A Counterpoint of View.* New York: Dodd Mead, 1982.

Doráti, Antal. *Notes of Seven Decades,* rev. ed. Detroit: Wayne State University Press, 1981.

Eisenberg, Evan. *The Recording Angel: Explorations in Phonography.* New York: McGraw-Hill, 1987.

Haggin, B. H. *Conversations with Toscanini.* New York: Doubleday, 1959.

Hart, Philip. *Conductors: A New Generation.* New York: Charles Scribner's Sons, 1979.

Heyworth, Peter, ed. *Conversations with Klemperer.* London: Victor Gollancz, 1973.

Horowitz, Joseph. *Understanding Toscanini: How He Became an American Culture God and Helped Create a New Audience for Old Music.* New York: Alfred A. Knopf, 1987.

Leinsdorf, Erich. *Cadenza: A Musical Career.* Boston: Houghton Mifflin, 1976.

————. *The Composer's Advocate: A Radical Orthodoxy for Musicians.* New Haven, Conn.: Yale University Press, 1981.

McClure, John. "For the Record: Leonard Bernstein in the Studio." In *Sennets & Tuckets: A Bernstein Celebration,* edited by Steven Ledbetter, 115–21. Boston: Boston Symphony Orchestra in association with David R. Godine, 1988.

Marek, George R. *Toscanini.* New York: Atheneum, 1975.

Matheopoulos, Helena. *Maestro: Encounters with Conductors of Today.* New York: Harper & Row, 1982.

Osbourne, Richard. *Conversations with Von Karajan.* New York: Harper & Row, 1989.

Parrott, Jasper with Vladimir Ashkenazy. *Ashkenazy: Beyond Frontiers.* New York: Atheneum, 1985.

Peyser, Joan. *Bernstein: A Biography.* New York: William Morrow, 1987.

Robinson, Paul. *Solti.* New York: Vanguard, 1979.

Rodzinski, Halina. *Our Two Lives.* New York: Charles Scribner's Sons, 1976.

Russell, John. *Erich Kleiber: A Memoir.* London: Andre Deutsch, 1957.

Sachs, Harvey. *Reflections on Toscanini.* New York: Grove Weidenfeld, 1991.

————. *Toscanini.* Philadelphia: J. B. Lippincott Co., 1978.

Schonberg, Harold C. *The Great Conductors.* New York: Simon & Schuster, 1967.

Schönzeler, Hans-Hubert. *Furtwängler.* Portland, Ore.: Amadeus, 1990.

Shirakawa, Sam H. *The Devil's Music Master: The Controversial Life and Career of Wilhelm Furtwängler.* New York: Oxford University Press, 1992.

Walter, Bruno. *Theme and Variations.* Translated by James A. Saston. New York: Alfred A. Knopf, 1946.

Wooldrige, David. *Conductor's World.* New York: Praeger, 1970.

RECORDING THE CLASSICS

was composed in Adobe Garamond
using Aldus PageMaker 5.0 for Macintosh
at The Kent State University Press,
printed by sheet-fed offset
on 50-pound Supple Opaque Natural Recycled stock,
notch case bound with 88-point binder's boards
in ICG Kennett book cloth,
and wrapped with dustjackets printed in
two colors 100-pound enamel
by Thomson-Shore, Inc.;
designed by Diana Gordy;
and published by
THE KENT STATE UNIVERSITY PRESS
KENT, OHIO 44242